Fundamentals of Writing for Marketing and Public Relations

Fundamentals of Writing for Marketing and Public Relations

A Step-by-Step Guide for Quick and Effective Results

Janet Mizrahi

First published in 2010 by
Business Expert Press, LLC
222 East 46th Street, New York, NY 10017
www.businessexpertpress.com

ISBN-13: 978-160649-173-7 (paperback)

ISBN-13: 978-160649-174-4 (e-book)

DOI 10.4128/ 9781606491744

A publication in the Business Expert Press Corporate Communication collection

Collection ISSN: 2156-8162 (print)
Collection ISSN: 2156-8170 (electronic)

Cover design by Jonathan Pennell
Interior design by Scribe Inc.

First edition: December 2010

10 9 8 7 6 5 4 3 2 1

Printed in the United States of America.

Abstract

This book will help anyone who wants to learn how to write or simply how to improve when writing for marketing and public relations. The author brings to light a fantastic, easy-to-follow guide that provides the basics needed to write promotional and informational materials. Written in an approachable style, this book contains helpful samples and useful checklists that will make even the most timid writers confident that they have represented their organization's message in a professional manner.

Inside you'll find an overview of the marketing and PR writing styles and chapters containing step-by-step guides to the most commonly used marketing and PR genres such as the following:

- News releases
- Newsletters
- Brochures
- Web copy
- Social media (blogs and microblogs)
- Pitch letter and media kit

Students studying business, marketing, public relations, or communication as well as small business owners and entrepreneurs will find this practical guide vital to their efforts to promote and inform various publics about their organization.

Keywords

Marketing style, press release, news release, brochure, blog, microblog, Tweet, newsletter, e-newsletter, web copy, web writing, website, public relations, marketing, writing, pitch letter, media kit, press kit, marcom

Contents

Illustrations

Figures

Tables

Acknowledgments

I am indebted to several people whose input has made writing this book possible. Debbie Gendel, my first editor and dear friend, boundless thanks for your knowledge, expertise, support, and professionalism. I am especially grateful for your help on the chapter covering social media and for your superb copyediting. And to Debbie DuFrene, my Business Expert Press editor, thanks for the advice, additions, and hand-holding. To LeeAnne Kryder, colleague and friend extraordinaire, *mille grazie* for your input and insights and for test-driving a chapter with your students. And thanks to my husband, Perry Hambright, for always saying yes when I need help.

CHAPTER 1

Basic Writing Guidelines

The key to writing well is to remember that writing is a process—a series of steps rather than a one-shot deal. Whether you write an email to a colleague or create content for a start-up company's website, your prose will be better and will take less time to compose if you look at writing as a series of tasks. Even if you suffer from writer's block or shudder at the thought of writing, I can promise that when you break down writing into several component parts, the result will be better and you will be less frazzled.

AWE Writing Method

The task of writing has three separate steps, for which I've developed an acronym: AWE, short for assess, write, edit. These three steps should be completed for every piece of writing that will be seen by another person.

Step One: Assess

Before your fingers touch the keyboard or you put pen to paper, assess the writing situation by defining your **audience and purpose**. I recommend making this step formal: Write down your answers. Many advertising and PR agencies use forms called project briefs, which writers complete for each writing task. (We'll discuss project briefs more completely in chapter 4.) They include, in part, the following criteria:

1. **Know your audience.** The language you use, the style in which you write, and the medium you employ are determined by who will read what you write. Use Table 1.1 to create a reader profile.
2. **Define your purpose.** The reason for writing any content falls into three basic categories: informing, persuading, and requesting.

Table 1.1. Audience Profile

Audience characteristic	Rationale
Age	Writing for children differs from writing for adults or teens. Our tone, word choice, and medium may alter greatly depending on the age of the reader.
Gender	Writing for an all-male audience will differ from writing for an all-female audience. Likewise, if the audience is mixed, we may make different language choices than we do for a homogeneous group.
Language proficiency	The reader's knowledge of English will affect your word choice, sentence length, and other stylistic elements.
Education level	We may be writing for an audience with a 10th-grade reading level or one comprised of college graduates. Each audience will have different expectations and needs, both of which the writer must be aware.
Attitude to- ward writer or organization	We must know if the audience is skeptical, frightened, pleased, or hostile toward the topic or the organization. Writers who antici- pate an audience's reaction write in a fashion that will support the document's purpose.
Knowledge of the topic	A document may be geared to people who are experts in a field or who know nothing about it. Even within an organization, several audiences will exist. The writer may emphasize different aspects of a topic depending on the readers' knowledge levels.
Audience action	What do you want your audience to do after reading? Click a link for more information? Call to take advantage now? You must have a clear vision of your goal in communicating for a document to be successful.

Informative writing includes instructions, notifications, warnings, or clarifications. Persuasive writing makes an impression, influences decisions, gains acceptance, sells, and recommends. Requests are written to gain information or rights and to stimulate an action.

Unless you define the desired outcome of the written task, you cannot achieve that task's objective. Are you writing a brochure to explain how to put up wallpaper or to convince a potential client to call a travel agent for more information? Are you issuing a press release to garner publicity for an event your firm is sponsoring or creating a newsletter to encourage your organization's members to participate? Whatever the form of communication, know what you want it to accomplish before you write.

3. **Research the topic**. Gather the information you need. Interview experts, search databases, or actually do what you're explaining in your writing task. Obtain whatever information you'll need *before* you begin writing. Nothing is more frustrating than being on a deadline and realizing that you do not have the information you need.

4. **Organize your information**. First have all the facts physically on hand. It's hard to manipulate 20 web pages on a screen at once, so print information when writing from multiple sources. On the printed page, highlight important points that must be included, remembering to reword anything you have taken from another source. It is plagiarism to use the exact wording of any copyrighted piece of writing without citing it even if the words are within quotation marks.

5. **Categorize your information into sections**. If you are writing a brochure about a bed-and-breakfast, put facts about the destination's location in one pile, information about the inn and its amenities in another, and directions to the locale in another.

6. **Outline** the information you have gathered using headings and subheadings.

This first element of the writing process—assessing—should take about 25% of the total time spent on the task.[1]

Step Two: Write

Many people think that good writing flows out of the brain, into the fingers, and onto the page. Nothing could be further from the truth. Professional writers know that writing, like any acquired skill, requires dogged persistence. The essence of good writing is rewriting. So enter the second step of writing knowing that it is not the last step. A draft by definition is not final.

The purpose of a **draft** is to transfer the information you have gathered onto the page. Begin by referring to the outline you've created, and write section by section, point by point. If you have trouble with one section, move to another. Your goal at this stage of the writing process is to put something down on paper (or on the screen) that you will revise later.

It's a waste of your valuable time to labor over any individual word or sentence as you write your draft; that word or sentence may be eliminated by the final version. If you cannot think of the precise word you need, leave a blank and return later to fill it in. If you are having difficulty wording a sentence smoothly, leave a bracketed space or perhaps type a few words as a reminder of the gist of what you want to say. The important point to remember is that a first draft is one of several stabs you'll take at this document.

Before you move to the next step, print a copy of your draft. But don't read it immediately. Let it marinate. It's too hard to edit our own copy immediately after we've written it. We need to let some time pass before we return to a draft so that we can be more objective when we edit.

This portion of the process should take about 25% of the total amount of time you work on the project.[2]

Step Three: Edit

I saw a great T-shirt at a meeting for the Society for Technical Writers. On the front was the word *Write* in boldface. Following that was line after line of the word *Edit*. The final boldface word at the end of the last line was *Publish*. Of course, the idea is that writing requires more editing than writing.

Global editing. Editing is a multistep process that begins by looking at the overall effectiveness of the piece. This is called global editing. As you read your draft, return to your audience and purpose analysis: Have you written a document that meets the needs of the audience while it accomplishes your purpose in writing? Does the document provide all the information end users will need to do what you want? Does it make sense? Is it well organized? If not, go back and make changes.

Local editing. Once you are certain that the content is correct and complete, it's time for **paragraph and sentence-level editing**, called local editing. This is where you'll need a good style guide (see the discussion "Writing Tools" later in this chapter), unless you are one of the few who has perfect recall of all grammatical rules. Begin by examining the effectiveness of each paragraph. By definition, a paragraph is a group of sentences about one topic; that topic is generally stated in the first sentence of a paragraph and is called a topic sentence. Good paragraphs have

unity, which means they stay on topic, so first check each paragraph for unity. Make sure your paragraphs aren't too long. In all marketing materials, we need to make sure our documents are reader friendly, and long paragraphs scare readers off.

Next check your paragraphs for **cohesion**, meaning that each sentence leads logically to the next. A common writing error is to jump from one idea to the next without providing a logical connection between those two ideas. Unless each idea expressed in a sentence logically segues to the next, your reader will not be able to follow. Writers link ideas in several ways:

1. Using transitional words and phrases. Transitions are broken down into types: adding information, contrasting information, comparing information, illustrating a point, and showing time.
2. Using pronouns that refer back to a specific noun.
3. Repeating key words to remind a reader of a central idea.

Once all paragraphs are edited, **examine each sentence**. Now is the time to nitpick grammar and stylistic elements. If you consider your knowledge level of grammar weak, don't worry. With the right tools and dedication, you can master the most important grammatical issues. Pay special attention to egregious errors such as the following:

1. Subject-verb agreement
2. Comma splices
3. Sentence fragments
4. Run-on sentences
5. Dangling modifiers

Dangling modifiers are phrases that confuse readers by saying something other than what is meant. They often appear in an introductory phrase at the beginning of a sentence but omit a word that would clarify meaning in the second part of the sentence. Look at the following sentence:

After finishing the copy, the website was difficult to understand.

The website did not finish the copy (a synonym for written material); therefore, the meaning is obscured. Perhaps this sentence should read,

After finishing the copy, the writer/reader found that the website was difficult to understand.

Next find every pronoun to make sure it agrees with its antecedent and that the noun to which it refers is clear. Make sure you have written numbers in the correct way, using numerals and spelling out numbers appropriately. Stay in the same verb tense.

As you edit, take some time to **read your copy aloud** and make marks next to areas that require editing. This is the single best way to improve your writing. Professional writing should sound natural. If you find yourself stumbling as you read your copy, the chances are good that you have a problem; your ears will not allow you to pass over stylistic elements that your eye will just ignore. Listen for frequent repetition of the same word; for short, choppy sentences; and for sentences that begin with the same word or phrase. Make sure your sentences have variety in length, going for a good mix of short, medium, and longer sentences. Note whether you have started too many sentences with *there is, there are, this is,* or *it is.* Overuse of this wordy construction is a red alert for any professional writer to rewrite. (See the "Avoiding Wordiness Checklist" at the end of this chapter.) Finally, make sure you have used words according to their denotations.

About 45% of the writing task is spent editing. This portion of the writing process is the most laborious, but it is also the most critical.

Proofreading. The final element of writing is proofreading—editing your copy for typos and spelling, capitalization, punctuation, and formatting errors. Begin by double-checking the correct **spelling** of names. Then **look at capitalization** of nouns and titles and be consistent. Consult a style guide or dictionary if you are unsure of what and when to capitalize.

Next make sure you've used words correctly. Some words look or sound similar but have entirely different meanings (e.g., affect/effect and complimentary/complementary). If you have included a phone number or a URL in the copy, determine both are correct by calling the number or checking the link.

A warning about using Microsoft Word's spell-check function: Spell check is far from foolproof. The omission of just one letter (say, the last *s* in *possess*) can change the word's meaning, and Word won't pick that up.

Posses is a word (the plural of posse), but it isn't the word you meant to use. Microsoft Word also won't find names spelled incorrectly or words not in its dictionary.

Proofreading for **punctuation** is critical. Proper use of commas makes a huge difference in a document's readability. Be especially on the lookout for inserting commas after introductory phrases and between two independent clauses joined by a coordinate conjunction. Likewise, tossing in a comma or semicolon haphazardly or omitting a comma or semicolon are common writing errors that affect readability. Both can slow flow and muddle meaning. Consider how the comma alters these two sentences:

That, I'm afraid, has not been the case.

That I'm afraid has not been the case.

The first sentence refers to a previous statement and conveys the meaning that an earlier statement is untrue. The second means that the individual claims to be unafraid.

Next examine your document's **format**. Adhere to guidelines for the genre in which you are writing. Remember that documents not only must be well written; they must be attractive on the page or on the screen to maximize readability.

Proofreading should take about 5% of the total time of the writing process.[3]

Refer to the "Editing and Proofreading Checklist" at the end of this chapter.

Marketing and PR Writing Style

Writing promotional materials requires a high degree of professionalism. After all, the words on the page represent an organization. Everything from a company's website to its brochures to an annual report reflects not just the writer who composes the materials but also the firm behind that writer. So when composing for marketing and public relations, the writer must pay attention to the following elements:

1. **Accuracy**. Being accurate is important for several reasons. First, creating marketing and PR materials is not only time intensive—it's costly.

If the material contains flawed information, the time and energy that went into production have been wasted. Second, inaccuracies show a carelessness that few businesses can afford in a competitive, global marketplace. Attention to accuracy is therefore paramount to marketing and PR writers.

2. **Avoiding gender, racial, and age bias**. The English language makes biases difficult to avoid. The best way to stay away from the he/she conundrum is to use the plural of a word. For example, instead of saying, *A manager tries to be well liked by his employees*, say, *Managers try to be well-liked by their employees*. To avoid racial or age biases, beware of stereotypes when composing. Even if the reference is complimentary, those to whom you refer will likely find that reference offensive.

3. **Clarity**. If the reader has to reread to understand anything in your document, you have not done your job. All PR materials need to be easy to read. Clarity comes from using words the audience will recognize and using those words correctly. Stay away from jargon or SAT-prep vocabulary. One way to check your work for clarity is to give your draft to someone who knows nothing about what you are writing. If that reader can understand the document, it is probably clear.

4. **Conciseness**. Readers need brevity. No one wants to wade through wordy prose to get to a point. See the "Avoiding Wordiness Checklist" at the end of this chapter for a list of wordy phrases you can easily learn to eliminate.

5. **Conversational prose with smooth flow**. The rhythm of any prose needs to be conversational and natural. The best way to achieve good flow is to read your copy aloud and keep amending or editing until you are able to read without hesitation. Use simple language in sentences that are not complex or convoluted. Make sure that your punctuation does not impede the reader by adding unnecessary halts and that you have inserted pauses that will aid understanding.

To make our prose more conversational, marketing and PR writers also use contractions when appropriate. Instead of *they will*, use *they'll*. We can also begin our sentences with *and* or *but*, which many English teachers taught as incorrect. Sometimes beginning a sentence with a conjunction gives prose just the right rhythm to create that highly desired conversational tone.

6. **Correctness.** Poor grammar and words used incorrectly make the writer and the organization appear ignorant and sloppy. To hone your grammatical skills, work with a grammar guide next to you. Consult it when you are unsure about any writing issue. Make use of Word's grammar and spell check, but do not rely on them solely. Familiarize yourself with the rules of writing. Correct grammar will clarify your writing, too.

Another way to work on grammar issues is to create a "Never Again" table. This is a three-column table (see Table 1.2) that lists a grammatical error, the rule that governs the problem, and a mnemonic device to remember the solution. When you keep a list of grammatical errors and refer to it as you compose, you will eventually learn to correct the problem. Keep adding and erasing errors until you no longer need to consult the chart.

7. **Parallelism.** Good writing often uses a device called parallelism, or parallel structure. Writers use parallelism instinctually because it appeals to our natural desire for symmetry. Parallelism matches nouns with nouns, verbs with verbs, and phrases with phrases: "For *faster* action, *less* stomach upset, and *more* for your money, use XX." Readers expect parallelism, especially in sets of two or three items. Using parallel phrasing sets up an expectation in the reader, and when used correctly, delivers a punch the reader will appreciate.

8. **Positive voice.** Positive voice uses affirmative words to make a point. For example, instead of saying, "We are out of green T-shirts," the marketing or PR writer would emphasize the positive and say, "Order any size of our orange and gray T-shirts." Avoid downbeat words or words than can convey a negative connotation, and

Table 1.2. Sample "Never Again" Grammar Remediation

Grammar problem	Rule	Mnemonic device
Its vs. it's	It's *always* = it is	The dog bites its tail because it's plagued with fleas.
Effect vs. affect	Effect = noun Affect = verb	Ibuprofen adversely affects my stomach, but the medicine's effect cures my headache.

rephrase in a positive way. Instead of "No coupons will be honored after May 1," say, "Coupons will be honored through April 30."

9. **Strong nouns and verbs**. Good writing uses nouns and verbs to do the heavy work and saves adverbs and adjectives for rare occasions. Instead of "Our brightly colored, twinkling lights will be reminders of the happiest, most memorable times you and your family will ever enjoy," say, "Our dazzling lights will twinkle their way into your family's memories." Replace "The fire was hot" with "The inferno blazed." Avoid using the most boring and overused verb in the English language: to be. Check your prose for usage of *is*, *are*, *were*, and *was*, and see if you can eliminate them by using a stronger, more specific verb. We can't entirely avoid adverbs, adjectives, or "to be," but we can be mindful of how often we use them.

10. **Sentence variety**. Sentence variety is linked to conversational prose and has two elements. The first is sentence beginnings. As you edit, look at the way your sentences begin. Do three in a row begin with "The"? Do two sentences within two paragraphs begin with "There are"? Avoid writing sentences that begin with the same word or phrase.

    The second way to attain sentence variety is to vary sentence length. Short, choppy sentences make prose annoyingly staccato. Natural-sounding prose combines short, medium, and longer sentences. One way to check your sentence length is to look at how the periods line up on your page. If you see a vertical or slanted line of periods, you need to alter some of the sentence lengths. This can be accomplished in several ways.

    • Join two sentences whose content is closely linked by embedding the gist of one sentence into another. For example, look at these two sentences:

        We will be closed Monday for Memorial Day. Memorial Day falls on May 30 this year.

      If we embed one into the other, we have a less repetitive, more concise sentence:

        We will close on Monday, May 30, for Memorial Day.

- Combine two sentences with a coordinate conjunction. The following sentences are unnecessarily repetitive:

  We guarantee delivery by Mother's Day if you make your purchase by May 8. All purchases made before May 8 will also be gift wrapped free of charge.

  Join the two sentences with a coordinate conjunction, and you tighten your prose.

  We guarantee delivery for Mother's Day if you make your purchase by May 8, and we'll even gift wrap your item for free.

- Add an alternate sentence beginning such as an introductory phrase to vary sentences.

  In the previous example, we could use this strategy to rewrite.

  If you make your purchase by May 8, we'll guarantee delivery by Mother's Day and will even gift wrap your item for free.

11. **Simple words**. Avoid jargon. Always, always, always choose the simpler, more recognizable word over the longer, showier one. Instead of *rhinovirus* say *a cold*. Opt for *email* over *electronic message*. In *utilize* vs. *use*, *use* wins! (Notice how the number of words and characters goes down with simpler words, too.)

12. **Shorter paragraphs**. Long paragraphs are appropriate for essays, but they have no place in promotional materials. Big blocks of type scare readers away. The longest paragraph should be no more than eight lines. Always be aware of how a paragraph appears on a page, and take pity on your audience—don't make them slog through dense prose.

13. **Tone and voice**. Writers must wear different hats and adjust their writing attitudes—sometimes called voice or tone—to the task at hand. Tone and voice are relayed with word choice and awareness of stylistic elements. Both are tied to the audience and purpose analysis; therefore, a piece's tone should be determined before writing begins. Most marketing and PR materials adopt a formal voice, which is controlled and objective. But some tasks may call for an informal tone in which you can be more personal and casual. Nevertheless, all professional writing should be courteous and avoid sarcasm.

Writing Tools

Just as a doctor wouldn't enter an examination room without a stethoscope or a carpenter wouldn't pull up to a job site without a hammer, no writer can be without the tools of the trade: a good dictionary, thesaurus, and style guide. Many excellent writing reference books are on the market, both in electronic and print format. I use both.

1. **Dictionaries**. Although I often visit Dictionary.com when I write, I also rely on my hard copy dictionary. Dictionaries in book format allow us to browse, and sometimes the writer will happen upon a word or meaning—something that doesn't occur when you use Dictionary.com.
2. **Thesauruses**. The same goes for the thesaurus. I find the thesaurus built into Word to be very weak. As a writer, I need to make the most out of the bounteous English language. A hard cover thesaurus is worth its weight in gold. I recommend *Roget's 21st Century Thesaurus*, edited by Barbara Ann Kipfer, PhD.
3. **Style guides**. Many good style guides are available. I recommend Franklin Covey's *A Style Guide for Business and Technical Communication*, 4th edition. It contains every grammar issue you'll ever encounter as well as a plethora of other relevant material. For a grammar guide, I use Diana Hacker's *A Writer's Reference*, 6th edition, but many excellent grammar reference books are available. And all PR writers should have the *AP Stylebook* by the Associated Press on hand.

The important thing to remember is to keep your tools nearby as you write. The more you use these reference books, the less you'll need them. You will internalize the rules of writing as you use them.

Conclusion

Writing doesn't have to be a dreaded chore. Breaking down writing tasks into stages can make the process more manageable and the end product more likely to accomplish its ultimate purpose. Writing for marketing and public relations requires a high degree of professionalism because it is used to present a company's face to the public. Grammatically incorrect writing or careless errors reflect poorly on an organization and the author. The writer who produces a professional end product is a valued member of any organization.

Avoiding Wordiness Checklist

✓	Wordy phrase	Wordy phrase examples	Solution	Solution examples
	Avoid beginning a sentence with *There are* or *It is.*	There are four points that should be considered. It is clear that cashmere is warmer.	Begin sentences with the true subject.	Consider these four points or Four points should be considered. Cashmere is clearly warmer.
	Avoid beginning sentences with *That* or *This.*	Choosing teams should be done carefully. This is because a good mix will generate better results.	Connect to previous sentence.	Choosing teams should be done carefully because a good mix will generate better results.
	Use *active voice* rather than passive.	Rain forests are being destroyed by uncontrolled logging.	Passive voice depletes prose of vitality and can almost always be rewritten in active voice.	Uncontrolled logging is destroying rain forests.
	Omit *that* or *which* whenever possible.	The water heater that you install will last 15–20 years.	Unless that or which is required for clarity, omit.	The water heater you install will last 15–20 years.
	Avoid prepositional phrase modifiers.	The committee of financial leaders meets every Tuesday.	Replace with one-word modifiers.	The financial leaders committee meets every Tuesday.
	Avoid conjugations of the verb *to be* (is, are, was, were, etc.).	New Orleans is one of the most vibrant cities in the U.S.	Replace with a strong verb.	New Orleans vibrates with activity like no other U.S. city.
	Tighten closely related sentences of explanation.	When hanging wallpaper, three factors need to be considered. The factors are X, X, and X.	Join closely related sentences of explanation with a colon to avoid repetitions.	When hanging wallpaper, consider three factors: X, X, and X.

Avoiding Wordiness Checklist (*continued*)

✓	Wordy Phrase	Wordy Phrase Examples	Solution	Solution Examples
	Tighten closely related sentences.	MRIs are used to diagnose many ailments. MRIs create an image of organs and soft tissues to diagnose.	Omit repetitious phrasing in second sentence.	MRIs diagnose ailments by creating images of organs and soft tissues.
	Tighten verb phrases with auxiliary + ing verbs	Management was holding a staff meeting.	Replace is, are, was, were, and have + verb with a one-word verb.	Management held a staff meeting.
	Avoid using *there is* or *there are* within a sentence.	When creating a mail list, there are many pitfalls.	Find an active verb to replace *there is* or *there are*.	When creating a mail list, many pitfalls exist.

Editing and Proofreading Checklist

✓	Item
	Document content is tailored to meet needs of audience and attains writing purpose
	Copy is edited for conciseness
	Body paragraphs have unity and cohesion and are shortened for visual appeal
	Transitions in and between paragraphs adequately link ideas
	Grammar is correct
	Punctuation is used correctly
	Copy has good rhythm and flow and uses a natural and conversational tone
	Sentences show variety in beginning and length
	Names are spelled correctly; phone numbers and URLs are accurate
	Words are used correctly
	Capitalization is consistent and adheres to specific stylebook guidelines
	Document adheres to specific genre formatting guidelines
	Document shows professionalism

CHAPTER 2

Writing News Releases

A news release—also widely referred to as a press release—is an organization's message written to appeal to news media outlets in hopes that those outlets will disseminate the message. That message can take many forms. It may be news about a recent hire, an employee's promotion, a product, or an event the company is sponsoring. News releases are often used to put a company's spin on bad news about earnings, product problems, or other events that reflect negatively on a business. News releases contain information that may be overlooked by the media but that the organization wants to publicize, or release. Both nonprofit and for-profit groups routinely use this form of public relations communication.

The purpose of the news release is simple: to convey a message to the masses without paying exorbitant advertising fees. It may originate from a university that wants to publicize winning a large grant, a nonprofit that is organizing a fund-raising event it hopes to publicize, or a business that is informing the public of a staff promotion, a new product, earnings, or a problem. The news release must walk the delicate line between serving the purpose of the issuer and the needs of the media.

Whichever type of organization you are writing for, it's important to understand how the media uses news releases. Broadcasters, digital media outlets, newspapers, and trade and consumer magazines cover a geographic area (think *Detroit Free Press*) or are designed to appeal to a specific niche (e.g., Lifetime Network or *Sports Illustrated*). News is gathered when reporters go to a scene of an incident (city hall, an accident scene, a new play, a sporting event), uncover facts, and report them.

Whether from the *Miami Herald* or CNBC, an editor chooses which stories to run and where or how they are played in the news vehicle. In newspapers, editors decide if news appears on the front page or is buried in the middle of the business section. On-air editors choose their lead news story and then allocate time to other features for television or radio broadcasts. Often times, however, editors need to fill a hole in their publication or broadcast; this is where the news release comes in. The news release provides editors with story ideas they may otherwise ignore. Editors are busy and do not want to give a business free publicity, so the savvy news release writer will give the editor a well-written, factual, and accurate piece of news that will be of interest to the editor's readers or viewers.

Although news releases are targeted to the media, many organizations also issue news releases that are intended for a different audience: corporate stakeholders. These releases are uploaded to a company's website and reside there to communicate company news to investors. They are written the same way as a news release that is geared to the media but are generally more promotional in nature.

Types of Releases

The majority of news releases contain "hard news," or news that is up-to-the-minute and serious in nature. Although all types of news releases contain the same elements, they are used to promote varying objectives. The following are commonly used hard-news releases:

1. **Publicity release**. This type of release announces information about a business, organization, product, or service that has news value to local or national media. A publicity release may announce internal promotions, upcoming or past events, new hires or appointments, awards, honors, and mergers or acquisitions.
2. **Product release**. These releases contain information that is generally targeted to trade publications and relate news about the introduction of a product, an addition to a line, or a modification or improvement to an existing product.
3. **Bad news release**. When an organization must tell the truth about a negative situation, it issues a bad news release. This document must always be straightforward about negative news, providing facts in an honest, forthright fashion to establish credibility with the media.
4. **Financial release**. The financial release disseminates information about a company's earnings or other information of interest to shareholders. While national media such as the *Wall Street Journal* or

ABC Nightly News may be interested in reporting news about large, publicly held organizations, local media also tend to report on firms headquartered in their distribution area.

5. **Feature release.** Sometimes an organization may wish to send a news entity a fully developed story that is neither late-breaking news nor serious. These kinds of stories are called features or "soft news" and require a different type of release. A feature release is not always timely; in fact, feature releases can often be used any time and are therefore called "evergreen." They are more creative than hard news releases and contain an idea for a feature story or the story in its entirety.

Writing for the Media

News releases are designed for both broadcast and print media. Whether sent in digital or print form, they are intended to be published or "picked up" by a news outlet such as a newspaper, radio station, magazine, or television news broadcast. Therefore, it is imperative that any news release is **newsworthy**. Yet there is a difference between the content in a news release and actual news. News releases are carefully crafted messages that promote a company's point of view, whereas news, in theory, must be more objective.

The news release must catch the eye of the editor with its newsworthiness and objectivity while also promoting the company's perspective. Newsworthiness is made up of two elements. The first are the **news values** or **five Ws and one H**—who, what, where, when, why, how—and are familiar to many people. Each of the news values is defined in Table 2.1. The second element of newsworthiness is seen in the criteria listed in Table 2.2. Writers use one or several of these elements or **angles** to emphasize newsworthiness.

When using a news release, the editor may reprint it as is or use the release as a starting point by assigning a reporter to follow up on the information provided in the release.

Table 2.1. News Values

News value	Definition
Who	Exact names and titles of people involved in an event
What	Major action or event stated in one sentence—often includes lesser actions or events related to major event
When	Time of event clearly stated
Where	Location of event
Why/how	Explanation of event including its context

Table 2.2. Elements of Newsworthiness

Newsworthy element	Explanation
Timeliness	Events are only newsworthy just before or directly after they occur
Prominence	Prominent figures and celebrities help publicize anything
Proximity	Local angle is a great "hook." (Editors say that if it happens to *our* community, it's news.)
Significance	Number and type of people who will be affected can make an item newsworthy
Uniqueness	Any bizarre or odd event will capture an editor's eye
Human interest	People like to read about other people, so this angle is also used to create interest
Newness	"Free" and "new" are key words that help generate interest in a news item

Style, Tone, Objectivity

Because news releases are written for the media, they must appeal to that discerning audience. First, a news release must never appear to be advertising—no editor wants to give free publicity! This means that the writing voice and tone should be objective rather than persuasive. As you compose a news release, think about a skeptical, cranky editor going through dozens or hundreds of these potential news items every week. Your job is to appeal to this editor's need for news to fill holes in the publication. Your need—to secure free publicity—is moot if your release does not make it past the editor's discriminating eye.

To appeal to the editor, keep the following in mind:

1. Keep word choice neutral and accurate. Avoid overblown adjectives and instead rely on strong nouns and verbs to make your point. Be factual, clear, and succinct.

2. Be correct. Writing for the media also means you must pay special attention to correctness. People in the media consider themselves writers, so news releases must be well written and tightly edited. Typos, misspellings, grammatical errors, or incorrect format will turn off an editor and minimize your chance of achieving your writing objective. The style guide the media uses (and consequently the style guide with which PR writers need to be familiar) is *The AP Stylebook*.

3. Decide if the release is hard news or more of a feature news story. News releases can be written in either a hard- or soft-news style. Hard news is timely and has immediacy. Soft news focuses on people or issues that affect people's lives. A soft news release (also called a *feature*) might take the form of a story about a child whose life was saved by a new drug, with the issuing company being the drug manufacturer.

News Release Submissions

News releases may be sent in hard copy or as an email. For optimal pick up, you should investigate how the organization you hope will use your news prefers to receive its releases. Many media outlets have guidelines for submitting a release.

Hard copy. Some organizations may prefer to receive news releases in hard copy format. Hard copy releases can run one to three pages, but most editors prefer concise releases of no more than two pages or three hundred words. If you are sending the release to multiple sections of a newspaper, be sure to include a note to each section editor that you have done so. When sending a hard copy release, issue it on company letterhead. Double space your text and indent each new paragraph.

Email. The majority of news releases today are sent electronically. These news releases are shorter than print news releases and generally fit on one or two screens. However, they adhere to the same rules as print releases except for the following:

1. The subject line of the email should contain the main idea of the release.
2. The release should not be an attachment; it should be contained in the body of the email.[1]
3. Company name (because it may not appear on letterhead) and contact information appear at the top of the electronic release and again at the end of the message. Some electronic news releases include an image such as the company logo at the top.
4. There should be one space above and below the headline.
5. Body copy is single-spaced with double-spacing between paragraphs, flush left.

The following link leads to an excellent example of an electronic news release issued by PR Newswire: http://news.prnewswire.com/DisplayReleaseContent.aspx?ACCT=104&story=/www/story/09–29–2009/0005102825&EDATE=.

Elements of the Hard News Release

The basic elements of a hard news release are as follows and are illustrated in Figure 2.1.

Headline ("head") and subhead. The purpose of the headline ("head") is to concisely capture the main idea of the release. Headlines are written with present-tense verbs and omit the articles "a," "an," and "the." The headline in a news release is crucial because if it does not clearly appeal to the editor and get the message across that an item is newsworthy, the release will be ignored. It is, in essence, the "sales pitch," although it must be worded to avoid sounding like an advertisement. Consider the difference in these two headlines. The first is overly persuasive, and the second is more objective.

1. *New Herb Guarantees Safe Weight Loss and Money-Back Guarantee*
2. *New Study Shows Herb's Effectiveness as Weight Loss Tool*

Headlines use clear, concrete language, avoiding vague, unspecific words. For best search engine optimization (SEO), the headline should contain key words that are repeated strategically throughout the release that echo the essence of the message. The headline should not mimic the lead paragraph; it should use different wording to get across the main idea of the release.

Secondary head. The secondary head ("subhead") is often a complete sentence that uses a full verb and the articles that are frequently omitted from headlines. The subhead assumes the presence of the headline and gives additional information that provides another layer of detail. It should not repeat the first headline and is not mandatory. Notice how the following subhead builds on the previous headline example.

Researchers find that thermogenic herbs rid the body of excess fluids.

Lead. The lead, or first paragraph, is the most important part of the release. Although many lead styles exist, the most common is the summary lead, which includes as many of the five Ws and one H as can fit without sounding awkward. In the lead we stress the release's news value, and we focus on an angle to make it newsworthy. (Refer to the previous list of newsworthy angles.) The order of information related in a lead should reflect the company's goal in writing the news release, but it must also keep in mind the needs of news organizations. Leads can be as many as 30–35 words, as long as they are clear.

Body (inverted pyramid style). The body of most news releases is one to two pages (occasionally up to three.) The body features relatively short paragraphs, although too many short, choppy paragraphs are discouraged. Like any good writing, the body of the document should be concise, clear, and accurate. Sentences should be varied and have good rhythm. However, news releases also possess the qualities of good journalism and use journalism's "inverted pyramid" style of writing. This means that the body is organized in descending order of importance; the most important elements are placed at the top, and the least important are placed toward the bottom. Editors use this style because, when deciding how much space or time to devote to an item, they cut from the bottom. By writing in the inverted pyramid style, we are helping the editor.

After the lead paragraph summarizes the release's newsworthiness, the second paragraph contains the next most important part of the news. What follows in subsequent paragraphs is less important, and so on. After all the points of the release have been covered, many releases add a paragraph that contains background information the reader may need to fully understand the significance of some aspect of the preceding story.

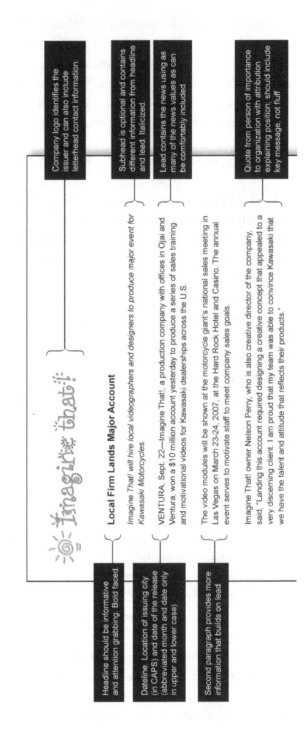

Company logo identifies the issuer and can also include letterhead contact information.

Subhead is optional and contains different information from headline and lead. Italicized.

Lead contains the news using as many of the news values as can be comfortably included

Quote from person of importance to organization with attribution explaining position; should include key message, not fluff

Imagine that!

Local Firm Lands Major Account

Imagine That! will hire local videographers and designers to produce major event for Kawasaki Motorcycles.

VENTURA, Sept. 22—Imagine That!, a production company with offices in Ojai and Ventura, won a $10 million account yesterday to produce a series of sales training and motivational videos for Kawasaki dealerships across the U.S.

The video modules will be shown at the motorcycle giant's national sales meeting in Las Vegas on March 23-24, 2007, at the Hard Rock Hotel and Casino. The annual event serves to motivate staff to meet company sales goals.

Imagine That! owner Nelson Perry, who is also creative director of the company, said, "Landing this account required designing a creative concept that appealed to a very discerning client. I am proud that my team was able to convince Kawasaki that we have the talent and attitude that reflects their products."

Headline should be informative and attention grabbing. Bold faced.

Dateline: Location of issuing city (in CAPS) and date of the release (abbreviated month and date only in upper and lower case)

Second paragraph provides more information that builds on lead

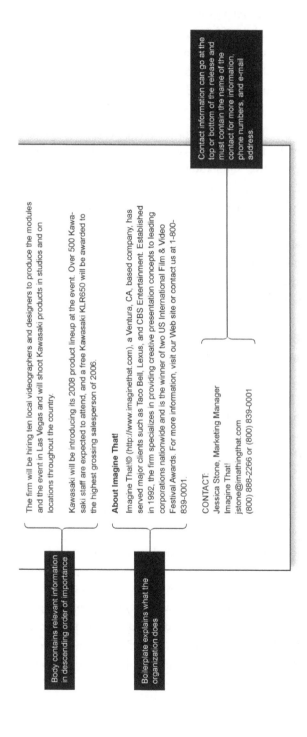

The firm will be hiring ten local videographers and designers to produce the modules and the event in Las Vegas and will shoot Kawasaki products in studios and on locations throughout the country.

Kawasaki will be introducing its 2008 product lineup at the event. Over 500 Kawasaki staff are expected to attend, and a free Kawasaki KLR650 will be awarded to the highest grossing salesperson of 2006.

About Imagine That!

Imagine That!© (http://www.imaginethat.com), a Ventura, CA, based company, has served major clients such as Taco Bell, Lexus, and CBS Entertainment. Established in 1992, the firm specializes in providing creative presentation concepts to leading corporations nationwide and is the winner of two US International Film & Video Festival Awards. For more information, visit our Web site or contact us at 1-800-839-0001.

CONTACT:
Jessica Stone, Marketing Manager
Imagine That!
jstone@imathingthat.com
(800) 888-2266 or (800) 839-0001

Body contains relevant information in descending order of importance

Boilerplate explains what the organization does

Contact information can go at the top or bottom of the release and must contain the name of the contact for more information, phone numbers, and e-mail address.

Figure 2.1. Sample news release.

Quotations. Most news releases contain a quotation from someone in the company in the third or fourth paragraph. For example, if the release is about a new hire or a promotion, the division manager may be quoted. If the release is about a new product, some other company official will make a statement that is quoted in the news release. Oftentimes these quotes are created by the public relations professional (in which case the quote is *always* approved by a superior.) The purpose of using a quote is to combine information the organization wants to impart with a more personal perspective. Quotations, which can be direct or paraphrased, add life to a story that a disembodied statement does not.

When quoting, the following should be taken into consideration:

1. Use the exact spelling and title of the person being quoted.
2. Use the first and last name the first time a person is named. Use only the last name thereafter.
3. Put commas and periods inside quotes.
4. Put other punctuation marks within the quotation marks if they are part of the quote. (Example: XYZ company spokesperson Jane Doe said, "Would we be willing to ship this package without worry? Yes, we would!")
5. Attribute each quote.
6. Introduce each person quoted. (Example: Mark Elliot, recipient of this year's award, said, "I am grateful for the opportunity to serve my community.")
7. Use "said" rather than "laughed," "snorted," and the like in news releases.
8. Use "according to" when referring to an inanimate source, not when referring to a person.
9. Use an indirect quote only when the speaker is inarticulate.

Boilerplate. The final paragraph of most news release is the "boilerplate." The boilerplate paragraph is a short summary (often including the company mission) that provides background information about an organization and may be 50–100 words. It may include what the company produces, the number of employees or outlets it has, its stock-trading information, or its corporate philosophy.

Elements of the Feature News Release

Feature news releases differ vastly from hard news releases. A feature release requires more creativity and finesse. Most of all, feature news releases require the PR writer to be familiar with the publication's readership and content.

Feature news releases are appropriate when a business wants to publicize a product or service using an angle. For example, if you work for a potato grower, you might want to send a feature release about new recipes, especially as a tie-in to a holiday such as Thanksgiving. If your organization manufactures prosthetic legs, you might issue a release about a patient who won a marathon running on your product. Editors are always interested in human-interest stories.

Features also highlight consumer news. For example, a utility company might issue a feature release, "10 Ways to Cut Your Gas Bill." A pharmaceutical company might send a release "How to Avoid Catching the Flu." Whatever the angle, always include the following elements when writing a feature news release.

Headline and subhead. Feature headlines need to be catchy and forecast the main idea ("Put Some Bite Into Teeth Cleaning"). The more you catch an editor's eye with a cute or captivating headline, the better your chances the editor will take a second look at your release. A subhead, as in a hard news release, is optional and should follow the same guidelines.

Delayed lead. Feature releases use a delayed lead instead of a summary lead. Instead of summarizing the news values in one sometimes-lengthy sentence, a delayed lead is a captivating hook to lure your reader to read on. It should last no more than a sentence or two and should end with a clear statement of the release's main idea. This statement is similar to a traditional feature story's "nut graf" (short for para*graph*), so called because it contains the essence or main point of a feature "in a nutshell."

The following is an example of a delayed lead with a nut graf.

Panting and sweat-drenched, a grinning Martha Bledsoe was one of hundreds who crossed the finish line at the recent Viceroy 500 Half Marathon. But what made Martha different was that she's 73.

[Nut graf] Seniors like Martha are part of a growing trend of elderly participants in athletic events once reserved for the young. But while these golden agers may be young at heart, their hearts aren't so young. And that means the active elderly must be extra careful when training.

The actual story will go on to discuss how the active elderly must be careful when training for a strenuous athletic event. The organization issuing the story would be promoting its product (perhaps a knee brace or special running shoes) in a subtle way.

Body. Unlike a hard news release, the body of a feature is not written in an inverted pyramid style. Instead, feature releases have an internal organizing element such as steps or events that occur over time. When composing a feature release, use quotations from a variety of sources, and follow the same quotation guidelines noted earlier. If the release provides URLs or phone numbers that consumers can use for more information, place these at the end of a paragraph in case an editor wants to omit them to save space.

Clever ending. The end of the feature release will also differ from the hard news release. Rather than the boilerplate, end the feature news release by returning to the catchy beginning. If you opened by describing a runner with a prosthetic leg pushing through the finish line, end by returning to that arresting image. Sum up the essence of the story by reminding the reader of the main points. Or end your feature release with a helpful URL that offers more information.

Using the previous example, we might end the release like this.

Martha says she plans to compete in a triathlon next year—with her twin sister. "It might be the first time in 70 years that I beat her."

Document Design

News releases include the following information and stylistic elements:

1. **Company address**: Name, street, city, zip code, phone number, fax, and website.
2. Words "**News Release**" typed in upper case figured prominently under company name.

3. **Contact name:** Name of person to whom questions about the release may be directed as well as the individual's phone number, email address, and fax.

4. **Release date:** If the release is meant to be distributed upon receipt, write "**FOR IMMEDIATE RELEASE.**" If the release is to be embargoed, write, "**EMBARGOED UNTIL 1–1–20XX.**" Releases are embargoed only when the issuer does not want that news to precede an announcement or, in the case of a scientific study, that study's publication in a peer-edited journal. Use caps and boldface for both immediate and embargoed release dates.

5. **Date of distribution:** The date the release is prepared. The date of distribution appears either under the release date or as part of the dateline.

6. **Headline:** Upper case, underline, and boldface are preferred.

7. **Dateline:** City and state of event's location followed by a dash that goes directly into the lead paragraph.

8. **Bullets.** Use plain bullets rather than numbers for lists or to itemize facts. Use bullets sparingly.

9. The word "**more**" must appear at the bottom of each page unless the release is only one page. A **page slug** (page 2 of 2) should appear at the top of the subsequent page, flush left.

10. Type in 12-point Times New Roman.

11. **Boilerplate.** Should appear after the news.

12. Use **end marks** "# # #" or "–30–" to indicate the end of the release.

13. **Visuals.** Photos that illustrate an element of your release are optional. If you include a photo, write a caption that explains what the photo illustrates.

Refer to the "News Release Checklist" at the end of this chapter as a guide when you compose your news release.

Conclusion

News releases have been labeled the workhorse of the PR professional. Although the media is in a state of flux, the news release is still a key ingredient in any public relations mix.

News Release Checklist

✓	News release item
	Complete contact information included: name, phone, email, address
	Headline is objective, tightly written, newsworthy; omits articles
	Subhead, if used, does not repeat news in headline; adds another layer of information and is written in a complete sentence
	Lead includes news values and main point of release; contains about 30 words
	Body is in inverted pyramid style, with more important news higher in story and details of news lower in story
	Quotations are not fluff but actual news put into the mouth of an appropriate company official. Quotations follow guidelines and punctuation rules
	Boilerplate contains enough information to adequately identify company scope, mission, and size
	Hard copy document is formatted correctly. Includes company letterhead with logo, contact information, release date, date of distribution, headline in caps and underlined/centered, dateline; body is double-spaced with indented paragraphs two and beyond; page numbering follows guidelines; uses end marks at end of release
	Electronic submission is formatted correctly. Includes email subject line with main idea of release. Release is cut-and-pasted into the body of the email. Contact information appears both at top and bottom of release. Company logo (optional) appears at top with one space above and below headline. Body copy is singlespaced with double-spacing between paragraphs

CHAPTER 3

Writing Newsletters

Newsletters are an effective way to build relationships with a group's stakeholders. Whether geared to supporters of a nonprofit, employees of an organization, members of a community, or any group with a shared concern, newsletters report on news or matters of interest in an entertaining, succinct style. Ranging in length from 2 to 20 pages, newsletters are comprised of regular topics called standing items and one-time, stand-alone pieces. The newsletter is often a significant component of an integrated marketing plan.

From the reader's perspective, newsletters can be eagerly anticipated or a waste of time, depending on the way they are written and the type of content they include. But because they can help members of a group feel included and informed, newsletters are an important tool in the PR writer's arsenal—when done correctly.

Types of Newsletters

Newsletters fit into several categories:

1. **Employee newsletters**, also referred to as "house organs," are one of the most common type written. Formatted like a mini newspaper, these newsletters are intended to foster goodwill among diverse workers. Employee newsletters offer news about the organization and notices of policy changes, and they feature stories that highlight the accomplishments of a department or an individual. An employee newsletter might include an interview with the CEO or report on a new product or an award received. Employee newsletters are valuable because they make staff members feel valued and part of a team.

2. **Member newsletters** are sent to people who have joined a group. These common newsletters feature articles of interest to people who

either support the organization currently (e.g., a paying member) or were part of a group at one time (e.g., alumni of a university). Clubs, professional organizations, and other groups use newsletters to keep members informed about events and opportunities for involvement. They are also a way to reach out to new members by illustrating what the group is doing.

3. **Community newsletters** are distributed to members who live in a specific area and who share concerns about their neighborhood.[1] These newsletters provide information about the quality of life in the area. For example, the local water district may send out a quarterly or biannual newsletter to all residents to update them on water quality issues.

4. **Special-interest newsletters** are designed to appeal to people who share a hobby, an interest, a perspective on an issue, or a trade.[2] Sometimes special-interest newsletters are available by paid subscription only, so relevant content is especially critical.

Newsletter Audience Analysis

Before designing the content for any newsletter, start by defining its audience. Are the potential readers employees? Paying members of an organization? Everyone living in a geographic area? Subscribers? Refer to the "Audience Profile" (Table 1.1) in chapter 1 to chart the specifics about your readers.

Next, assess the audience's knowledge level of the topic and its diversity. For employee and member newsletters, the audience may know a good deal about the organization. Depending on the organization's size, the audience may vary by gender, age, duration with the group, and position within the group. For community newsletters, the writer will need to take into consideration the various education levels of the readership. All these particulars should be addressed when selecting newsletter article content and writing style.

People who subscribe to newsletters expect valuable information on a specific topic. For example, the *Kiplinger Letter* forecasts business and economic trends and is read by a wide swath of business professionals. The *Mayo Clinic Health Letter* contains articles on medical and health issues geared to a lay audience. Whoever your readership, you will need to know as much as possible about readers' knowledge of your group or topic to create an effective newsletter.

Newsletter Purpose and Frequency

Once you have determined the newsletter's readership, think about what you want the newsletter to accomplish. Is your purpose to urge members of your group to become more involved? Do you want to keep readers updated about your organization's accomplishments? Are you sharing a new way to work on a hobby? Whatever your goal, a newsletter's function does not change with each issue, so it's important to be clear about your strategic purpose before designing the newsletter.

That being said, most newsletters are informative. Sometimes the purpose of that information is to simply add to the reader's knowledge. Other newsletters will use information as a way to encourage people to buy a product or service. Whichever is the case, writing to inform is different in style and tone than writing to persuade. We'll discuss the way to write articles for newsletters next, but it's important to remember that a newsletter's content needs to be worth spending time on. Articles cannot be perceived by your audience as "filler" or fluff.

Newsletters publish regularly, whether that is weekly, monthly, or quarterly. Since putting together a newsletter requires time and therefore a financial commitment, be realistic about how often you can produce a newsletter that will be eagerly anticipated. Then stick to the schedule.

Print Versus Online: Pros and Cons

It is common to see both print- and electronically published newsletters. Each has its benefits and drawbacks.

Hard Copy Newsletters

Hard copy newsletters continue to be used for several reasons. For one, many people enjoy receiving subscription publications in the mail. Because hard copy newsletters are printed on sturdy paper, they have almost the same staying power as a magazine and can be kept for future reference. Print newsletters are not always mailed; they can be distributed at various pick-up locations where members and nonmembers alike can have access to them. And of course, print newsletters are essential if your readership does not have Internet access.

The primary negative of print newsletters is the expense. Paper, printing, and mailing all add up to a hefty bill (and are eco-unfriendly), and if the newsletter is published frequently, those costs can be prohibitive. Secondary negatives exist as well. If mailed, print newsletters take longer to receive than electronically delivered ones. Keeping addresses up to date can be time consuming. And finally, print newsletters require camera-ready layouts. Whether a staff member has the knowledge to use a newsletter template or a graphic designer has to be hired, the print newsletter must be delivered to the printer ready to be printed.

Electronically Distributed Newsletters

E-newsletters are frequently used as a marketing tool to drive customers to a buying opportunity, to keep membership updated about an organization's events, or to encourage participation in a group's activities. They are fairly inexpensive to produce, although the amount of time writing and keeping addresses updated remains the same as with a print newsletter. E-newsletters have the potential to influence a huge number of people, thus increasing the organization's reach.

However, there are definite downsides to e-newsletters. It's easy to ignore an email; busy people delete emails without giving them a second thought, and spam filters may automatically remove your newsletter from a recipient's inbox. If the reader bothers to open the email, click-through rates vary. When I wrote an e-newsletter, we were thrilled when an article had a 16% click-through rate. Still, there is every indication that e-newsletters have become a fixture in the marketing mix.

Electronically distributed newsletters take several forms and are sometimes called e-zines or e-newsletters.[3] One type of e-newsletter is a plaintext version. Plaintext newsletters are sent to an email address and usually include links to a series of articles that the reader can scroll down to peruse. Oftentimes the plaintext newsletter will use the article's headline and a brief description or hook with a link to the full text. If articles are short enough to fit on a single screen, they may be shown in their entirety. Plaintext newsletters do not include visuals unless the link takes the reader to a fully operational website.

An e-zine newsletter resides on a website. Sometimes subscribers are made aware of a new issue of the newsletter via an email notification. Old issues are generally archived on the site so readers can refer to them. E-zines are read the same way as a website and can therefore include as many of the bells and whistles available with HTML as the publishers deem necessary.

Another type of electronic newsletter is an HTML version sent to an email address. These newsletters contain visuals and graphic devices plaintext does not allow, so they are visually interesting. But they are dependent on the end user's computer capabilities and may take a long time to load.

Figure 3.1 features the front page of an electronically distributed newsletter. At a hefty 20 pages, this yearly newsletter is easy to navigate, uses art effectively, and engages its stakeholders. Though its articles do not adhere to journalistic style, they contain information that will appeal to its readership.

To examine the newsletter in its entirely, go to http://ccber.lifesci .ucsb.edu/newsletter/CCBERVolume5/vol005_page_01.php.

Newsletter Contents

Although some newsletter material is gathered using traditional research methods, most information you'll need will have to be collected by conducting interviews. Learning how to interview and how to be a good reporter is the first step to writing your newsletter.

Interviewing

All newsletter articles require the writer to conduct interviews to gather the information necessary to write. Interviewing can be broken down into three parts: before, during, and after the interview.

Before interviewing someone, set up a convenient time and place for the meeting. Do as much research on the situation or person before your meeting so you appear well prepared. Come armed with a list of questions you believe your readership will expect you to ask. Devise

THE NATURE PRESS
CHEADLE CENTER FOR BIODIVERSITY AND ECOLOGICAL RESTORATION

In this Issue

Previous < 1 > Next

Our successful journey has been due to the incredible efforts by CCBER staff, faculty, student interns, and volunteers, whose numbers continue to grow.

CCBER provides valuable opportunities for under-graduates to integrate their educational objectives with work experience under the guidance of knowledgeable mentors.

Director's Foreword

Jennifer Thorsch

This has been a record year for fundraising and initiating new projects at CCBER!

Our successful journey has been due to the incredible efforts by CCBER staff, faculty, student interns, and volunteers, whose numbers continue to grow. CCBER continues to expand and develop new initiatives to address our main goals of education, research, collections and ecosystem management, and public service.

Our excitement began in May 2009 when we learned that CCBER had been awarded a two-year Biological Research Collections grant from the National Science Foundation to install a new compact storage system in the herbarium and curate the higher plant and algae specimens. A generous matching gift from the Cheadle family allowed us in December to purchase and install a state of the art system with increased capacity for future collection growth. We also were very fortunate to hire two local consultants, Dieter Wilken and Mary Carroll, to assist with the project. Two dedicated graduate students, one undergraduate student, and one volunteer are also working on the project. The grant has also stimulated a renewed interest in the CCBER plant and algae collections by students (current and former), California based consultants, and faculty such as J.R. Haller, whose extensive pine collection is housed at CCBER.

The CCBER herbarium has approximately 100,000 specimens that are being examined for damage, conservation needs, and nomenclatural updates. Many specimens still need to be mounted on archival paper with their associated data, which is extremely time consuming. As part of this effort, CCBER launched a new curatorial internship program this spring to recruit interested undergraduate students to assist with numerous curatorial activities. We had over twenty students apply for the internship! Under the direction of CCBER staff and faculty, the students are cleaning and organizing plant anatomy slide collections, mounting specimens, curating the algae collection, and working with our archivist on some of CCBER's photograph collections.

David Chapman moves the algae collection into the new herbarium compact storage cabinets.

Previous < 1 > Next

Figure 3.1. CCBER e-newsletter front page.

Source: http://ccber.lifesci.ucsb.edu/newsletter/CCBERVolume5/vol005_page_01.php

shorthand for words you know you'll use during the interview so you can take notes quickly.

Dress appropriately for your interview, and show up on time. As you talk, be sure to develop rapport with your subject. Be friendly but professional. You may tape an interview only if the interviewee gives you permission, but some people may not be as forthcoming if they see a recorder. Otherwise, be ready to take notes quickly and accurately. Some people use their computers to take notes. If you take a laptop, be sure to continually make eye contact with your subject. Don't worry about correct spelling, but do be sure you have plenty of battery power. Always have a backup to your computer—bring a notepad!

Begin an interview with easy questions: correct spelling of the name, length of time with the organization, title, and the like. Don't interject your opinions; your job is to elicit information from the interviewee. Use a good mix of open- and close-ended questions. Open-ended questions leave subjects free to digress or give opinions. A typical open-ended question would be, "What do you like best about your position?" A close-ended question elicits a very brief answer. Asking someone, "Do you like being president of the club?" can only produce a yes or no answer. Your objective is to gather as much information as possible so you have material that will allow you to write the most vibrant article possible.

If you will be asking difficult questions, wait until after you have gathered answers to your other questions. It's possible the interview will take a less-pleasant turn after delicate questions have been posed or that the interview will even end, so never begin with an uncomfortable question. Preface the question with, "I know our readers will want to know . . ."

At the end of every interview, ask if you may contact your interviewee later in case you have questions. You generally have one shot at a backup call, so gather all your questions beforehand.

After the interview, transcribe your notes immediately so the meeting is still fresh in your mind. The sooner you fill in holes, the better. Finally, you may want to send a thank you note, and let the person know when the newsletter article will run.

Writing Newsletter Articles

Newsletters combine standing and one-time items. *Standing items* are recurring articles, similar to a column in a newspaper. A standing item for a newsletter might be a president's letter, an employee-of-the-month feature, or a spotlight on a department. *Sporadic items* are one-time articles that deal with news that only will occur once. For example, a house organ may have a one-time article about the company picnic or a new employee benefit. A member newsletter might feature a one-time article reporting on the results of an annual marketing survey.

Newsletter articles can be broken into three basic styles: inverted pyramid, feature articles, and news briefs. Both news and feature-newsletter articles tend to be short, about three hundred words. News briefs are one to two sentences.

The **inverted pyramid article** mimics a typical news story reporting on an event that is about to occur or has happened in the immediate past. Referred to as "hard news," these types of articles require a serious or objective tone. Articles appearing in subject-specific subscription newsletters use this style almost exclusively.

Inverted pyramid articles begin with a summary *lead* that answers the basic news values of who, what, where, when, and why or how. The summary lead is the article's first paragraph and contains the gist of the entire story. The lead sentence is often long, up to 35 words. The remainder of an inverted pyramid article consists of facts written in descending order of importance that explain the main idea voiced in the lead. These facts are written in paragraphs of two to three sentences. Keep sentences on the short side; 20 words should be the maximum length.

The best way to attack writing an inverted pyramid article is to first write down all the facts, one per line. You will have a list of sentences. Then hone in on the main point that can be phrased in 25–35 words. One way of finding the lead is to look for a quotation that backs up the main point. Next, go through the remaining facts. Number them in importance as they pertain to illuminating the main point. The last point should be the least important fact. Inverted pyramid stories do not have formal endings; they just end with another fact.

Inverted pyramid stories attribute information to a source. Information coming from inanimate sources such as studies, organizations, or databases is attributed with the phrase "according to." Information coming from people is attributed using "says" or "said" and may be paraphrased or directly quoted. Using direct quotes gives articles objectivity because the information is being reported in the words of the individual quoted. Each time a new person is quoted, a new paragraph is used. (See chapter 2 on "News Releases" for more guidelines on using quotations.)

To attain objectivity, inverted pyramid stories should avoid a writer's voice. Objectivity is achieved by using words that are not loaded or that show opinion. ("Sadly, crafters who rely on this method will be woefully disappointed.") Inverted pyramid stories should also be wary of using the second-person construction (using "you")—this usually means the author has not found the appropriate noun. Speaking directly to the reader may be appropriate in some articles, but inverted pyramid stories do not fall into this category.

Feature articles are stories that go beyond the facts of news and often put a human face on an event or organization. They may take the form of a Q & A, a behind-the-scenes look at a business or an event, a how-to, or a testimony. In newsletters, many features are profiles of members or leaders of the organization. Features differ in tone and style from inverted pyramid articles; they are lighter and brighter and can have a slant or angle. Using narrative techniques, features often supplement our understanding of an event or organization by showing how it affects people.

Features begin with a *delayed lead* that entices the reader with a hook. In a few sentences, the lead uses a *double entendre*, an unexpected question, or a catchy anecdote that epitomizes the main point. Some features begin with a scene setter, or a description that leads us to the main point. For example, if the feature is about an individual, the writer may lead with a description of that person's workplace:

Walk by Marsha Brook's cubicle and you can't help but notice the walls covered in souvenirs. From the plush Peruvian llama atop her file cabinet to the photograph of a dogsled race in Alaska, Marsha's distinctive workspace looks more like a travel agency's than a market analyst's.

That's because when Marsha isn't collecting data at XYZ Inc., the veteran traveler is working toward her goal of visiting every country in the Western Hemisphere.

That second paragraph is called the nut or *nut graf* because it contains the article's *focus* in a nutshell, as we discussed in chapter 2. When using a delayed lead (as compared to a summary lead), the article's main point must appear close to the beginning of the story or the reader will become confused. Features don't ramble or simply report facts in a linear fashion. They tell a story with a beginning, a middle (the body), and an end. The nut graf should be the story's angle, or the approach the writer has taken to report the information contained in the story.

If the lead of a feature hooks the reader with a cute or catchy description or anecdote, the body contains the details that explain and amplify the lead. Similar to making points in an essay, the body of a feature is a narrative that is organized in a logical way. In features, *quotations* are sprinkled throughout to drive home a point. As narratives, features also use description or "color" to draw a picture in words. Features use anecdotes—short stories that illustrate a point—as a way to explain a key point or to add life to a story. Finally, features often contain background information a reader may need to fully understand the story's impact.

A feature has a formal conclusion called a *kicker*. Simply put, a kicker returns to the lead to complete a story's circle. In our previous example of Marsha Brook, our kicker might return to a photograph or the cubicle:

Come August, don't be surprised if you see a new piece of memorabilia on Marsha's cubicle wall. She's off to Uruguay next week.

The kicker concludes the story and gives the reader a sense of completion.

News briefs are usually one-paragraph descriptions of events, products, or other items. They summarize main points in a tightly written, well-constructed, easy-to-read blurb. Some newsletters feature many news briefs on one page. The important point to remember when writing news briefs is to be concise; excise every extra word but be sure to include all necessary information.

Writing Headlines

All articles must have a headline. Good headlines grab a reader's attention but do so in a way that doesn't mislead or confuse. Some tips for writing headlines follow:

1. Include the article's main idea.
2. Use strong nouns and verbs in active rather than passive voice.
3. Avoid "to be" verbs if possible.
4. Write in truncated language that omits articles and prepositions.
5. Have fun with feature headlines but do so in a way that still conveys the article's main point.
6. Read your headline aloud to hear its rhythm and to make sure it flows.
7. Create interest by using colorful, powerful language.

Some articles also include a subhead, or a *deck head*. Deck heads come after a headline, are often italicized, and are written in a complete sentence that builds on the information in the headline. Deck heads never repeat the news contained in the headline.

Art and Cutlines

All newsletters that go beyond text-only format should include art. Readers' eyes immediately go to any visual. They will look at the art, read the caption, and then if interested, go on to read the article. Avoid clip art if at all possible and instead use photographs. Be sure to get permission to use photography; it is illegal to download images from the web without permission or paying a fee.

Captions or *cutlines* do not point out the obvious ("Garth Veyda smiles at coworker Arlene Goodwin") but instead reflect what a photograph illustrates ("Manny Dodds from finance and Alisa Bales from marketing compete in the balloon-tossing contest at last week's company picnic.") Avoid using judgmental words that characterize a photograph ("horrendous" or "ecstatic") or assuming you know what an individual in a photograph thinks or feels ("Candelaria Lopez loves striking out her boss, Marcus Weil.") Always be sure you have spelled names correctly, and be concise.

Content Layout

To achieve the best readership levels for your newsletter, the placement of articles requires some strategic thinking. Following are some guidelines to keep in mind as you design articles.

Print Newsletter Layout

A print newsletter should take space into consideration. Length of articles, where to place art (photographs, charts, diagrams, etc.), and size of headlines are all dictated by the amount of space. If designed as an 8½ × 11" mailer, half or one-third of a page must be allocated for the mailing address. The front page of a print newsletter must include a banner with the publication's name or logo, the volume and issue number, the publication date, and an index with a table of contents as is illustrated in Figure 3.2. Two main stories with art should appear on page 1. These stories may need to "jump" to an interior page.

Happy faces, varied column width, and use of color make this newsletter approachable and engaging.

The inside pages of the newsletter contains the masthead, which is a box with the names of the publisher, editor, and perhaps contributors. It may also include an address and other publishing information. The content of the articles on the inside pages is up to the editor's discretion. Inside stories may include a letter from the president or CEO, announcements, short news briefs, Q & As, or a spotlight feature on an individual. It is common to see pull quotes in a newsletter. Pull quotes are quotes taken from an article that epitomize a main point. They are usually boxed, bold-faced, and in a larger font size than the body copy.

Many print newsletters use the top half of the back page for mailing information: the sender's and recipient's addresses and postage. The space below the fold is often reserved for a calendar of the organization's upcoming events. If you choose to place an article on the back page, it should fit the space exactly. Avoid placing jumps from inside articles on the last page.

The *AHA!* Summer Newsletter 2010

www.ahasb.com

Co-directors: Jennifer Freed, PhD, MFT, and Rendy Freedman, MFT

The Academy of Healing Arts for Teens (AHA!) is a project of the Family Therapy Institute, a nonprofit founded in 1980. AHA! is dedicated to the development of character, imagination, emotional intelligence, and social conscience in teenagers. All contributions are tax-deductible.

Leonor Reyes (right), director of the Isla Vista Teen Center, presented the Youth Agency Award to AHA! program director Isis Castañeda (left), and co-founders Rendy Freedman and Jennifer Freed (with award).

A Year of Challenges and Triumphs

AHA! named Youth Agency of the Year

The City of Santa Barbara selected *AHA!* to receive the 2010 Youth Agency Award, presented at the 9th Annual Santa Barbara Youth Leadership Awards Banquet on May 24. In making the award, the City noted that *"AHA!* has been recognized as faithfully living up to its mission to develop strong character in teens. Your program and your passionate staff have contributed to widening the imagination and conscious awareness of many teens. Additionally, *AHA!* has contributed to the advancement of adult professionals who work with teens. Truly, *AHA!* has been an inspiration for both teens and adults. We appreciate your contribution to the Santa Barbara community."

Serving over 800 teens in 2009-10

AHA! is now delivering its social and emotional intelligence curriculum to every freshman at Carpinteria and San Marcos High Schools, to several groups at Santa Barbara High, including a hand-selected group of highly at-risk teens; to students at three La Cuesta Continuation High Schools, and to students at Santa Barbara Junior High. In all, we served more than 700 teens in-school this year, and more than 100 teens after-school and over the summer.

"The most important thing I have learned is how to appreciate myself and others and how to control my feelings."—A SMHS 11th grader

"I've learned to listen to others' points of view even if you are very against it."—A SMHS 9th grader

Why social-emotional intelligence?

A growing body of research documents the importance of social and emotional learning (SEL) to students' personal and academic success and to the creation of a school climate conducive to learning. (When the brain is flooded with stress hormones very little learning can take place.)

The Collaborative for Academic, Social, and Emotional Learning (CASEL) reports that "In a quantitative review of 43 school-based SEL studies, SEL programs significantly decreased the number of suspensions and expulsions while improving school attendance, students' attitudes towards school, students' grades, and performance on

AHA!
111 E. Arrellaga St.
Santa Barbara
California 93101
882-2400, ext. 108
www.ahasb.com

Do you have a heart of gold?
(See inset page)

Figure 3.2. AHA print newsletter front page.

Electronic Newsletter Layout

An electronic newsletter's format varies depending on which format is used. In text-only e-newsletters, a list of all articles generally appears at the top of the screen. Text-only newsletters require the reader to scroll down to read individual articles or to arrive at the live link that will take the reader to the entire article. Readers of text-only newsletters will only click through to articles of interest. If your e-newsletter is in HTML, decide which stories are most likely to draw in readers and put those at the top. Remember to think of the audience's needs, not the organization's. You may want the reader to jump right to your special offer, but that is probably not the primary reason your reader is receiving and enjoying your newsletter.

If your newsletter is housed at a website, you'll want to have tabs across the top and links along the left side that take readers to regular, standing items. Readers don't like scrolling down, so keep articles short, around 300–400 words. Your home page should have an index of the articles in each issue, and in that index, you can add links to articles that do not fit into categories under your tabs.

Newsletter Design Basics

With the plethora of templates for both print and electronically produced newsletters, the writer might not give design much thought. Marketing materials, however, need to emphasize readability, and a document's appearance contributes to how copy is read. The following is a broad overview of some design basics that can be applied to creating your newsletter.

Print Newsletter Graphic Design

Most print newsletters use the 8½ × 11" page layout because this common size is easily stored in a binder. This size can also be used in a horizontal or vertical format. The number of pages is determined by the budget and the amount of information that needs to be communicated. A short newsletter is four, 8½ × 11" pages, but the page count can increase by two- or four-page increments.

The 8 ½ × 11" page must be divided into columns. Avoid wide columns; try to keep character count to 45 for a two-column format and 36 for a three-column design. (A character is a space, punctuation mark, or a letter.) If you justify margins, use hyphens to break up words rather than the awkward spacing caused by keeping words whole. A ragged right column is not as tidy looking as a justified column, but it's easier to read than justified columns without hyphens. Choose no more than two font styles; use a sans serif font such as Calibri, Verdana, Arial, or Helvetica for headlines and a serif font such as Cambria, Times, or Times New Roman for the body copy. Single-space for best readability, and double-space between paragraphs. There is no need to indent paragraphs when double-spacing. It is worth noting Word's newer 1.5 line spacing. Some prefer its more open appearance, but if you are at all conscious of space, you'll want to stick to single-spacing.

It makes sense to unify your newsletter look and feel with the rest of your marketing materials, so make sure that the colors and fonts you choose work with, not against, your other printed pieces. Select a color scheme and stick to it, working with one or two complementary colors that blend with the shade of the paper. For example, you may choose royal blue boldface for headlines and a gold band of color going across an antique white page. Use black for body copy type and avoid colors that will be hard to see or that are hard on the eyes (yellow or fuchsia). If your budget allows, print your newsletter using the full spectrum of colors (called four-color). This will allow you to print color photographs, which adds liveliness to a publication.

Graphic devices—boldface, italics, underlining, boxes, shading, rules, and bullets—should be applied consistently and sparingly. Remember that graphics are symbols used to communicate visually. For example, boldface draws attention to words. A rule separates one item from another. Italics tell a reader that a word deserves special attention. A shaded sidebar next to a longer story links that information to the adjacent piece but separates it at the same time. Bulleted points list items so the writer doesn't have to be repetitive. It's usually unnecessary to use two graphic devices on any one item; to boldface and underline a headline, for example, would be redundant.

Electronic Newsletter Graphic Design

Writing for the computer screen differs from writing for a printed page. When preparing your electronic newsletter, use these tips:

1. Keep line width to 70 characters maximum per line. Tracking more than 70 characters diminishes readability.
2. Use a sans serif font like Verdana. These clean, modern fonts produce a clearer image on the screen than serif fonts.
3. Be aware of color use for background and font. White type against a black background should be used sparingly, not for entire pages of content. Avoid colors that will distract from the copy.
4. Take advantage of space, and supplement your copy with images that add interest to your newsletter.

Your electronic newsletter's appearance is just as important as its content, so take some time to examine existing newsletters for ideas.

Conclusion

Newsletters remain one of the best ways to reach your constituency. While print versions are still popular, easily uploaded online newsletters will only become more prevalent. Adding a newsletter to your marketing and public relations plan will enhance your company's image and keep your stakeholders involved.

Newsletter Resources

Creating a Usable Electronic Newsletter In-House
http://www.stcsig.org/usability/newsletter/0301-enews.html
Free HTML Email Templates
http://www.mailchimp.com/resources/templates/
Free Management Account and Templates for 30 Days
https://www.mynewsletterbuilder.com/
How to Create a Newsletter—Free Script
http://www.2createawebsite.com/enhance/create-newsletter
.html
Create an Email Newsletter in Word
http://office.microsoft.com/en-us/word-help/staying-in-touch
-with-customers-create-an-e-mail-newsletter-in-word
-HA001045106.aspx

CHAPTER 4

Writing Brochures

Brochures have a permanence that makes them important to the promotional mix. Used to inform or to persuade, brochures provide readers with valuable information while conveying a sense of a company's professionalism and stability. Brochures proliferate every walk of life, from the doctor's office to a hotel lobby. When an organization wants to make itself and its offerings known or needs to explain a process, it produces an attractive, informative brochure.

Brochure Audience Analysis

Many brochures are aimed at an external audience that has either requested or seeks more information about a product, service, task, or an organization. A couple may request a brochure about a time-share; a small business owner may examine a brochure about a bookkeeping service; a homeowner may pick up a brochure that describes how to lay tile. In large organizations, brochures may be produced for an in-house audience to provide information about benefits, procedures, or opportunities.

Whatever the case, writers must start with a clear picture of the brochure's end user. Is the potential reader a new mother who needs information about when to vaccinate her baby or a possible client wishing to examine the qualifications of a consultant? Either way, the writer must be acutely aware of the reader's English proficiency and knowledge of the topic. When sitting down to create a brochure, the first step must be to develop a thorough audience profile.

Often a brochure is part of a major promotional program. In that case, the organization has likely invested in marketing surveys that produce detailed information about the consumers and their attitudes, including a *demographic and psychographic profile*. This information is crucial for the writer to produce the kind of copy that will push the consumer to react to the product offering. With or without a marketing survey, writing effective brochures requires a thorough understanding of the target customer's *needs and wants*, and its copy must appeal to those distinct requirements. If you have to, conduct your own small survey. You may also want to consult the "Lifestyle Market Analyst" published by SRDS, which provides buyer profiles.

Refer to chapter 1 to prepare an in-depth audience analysis before proceeding to write your brochure.

Brochure Purpose

A brochure's purpose also must be clarified before beginning to write. Is its goal to lure high-end buyers to a new housing development's groundbreaking event? Does the brochure need to explain to patients what to expect after rotator cuff surgery? Or must it provide the nuts and bolts about a club or organization?

When thinking about the purpose of a brochure, it is helpful to understand that brochures fall into two main categories.

Informational brochures describe a procedure (such as how to install wallpaper) or provide information about an organization, a condition, or a topic (e.g., an "Education Abroad Program at a University" or "How to Cope With Depression"). These types of brochures are practical and efficient.

Persuasive brochures are written with the objective of selling a product, service, or idea. Because they are produced by the company selling the product, persuasive brochures highlight only the best points about whatever is being sold. Still, persuasive brochures work best when information is presented in objective language without sounding "salesy."

If writing a persuasive brochure, the writer must know where it fits into the promotional mix or selling cycle to decide on the type of information to include and what writing style to employ. A stand-alone piece, for example, must contain all the information the reader needs to complete the desired action. A brochure that is part of a series may need to repeat certain information that appears in all the brochures.

How a brochure is used will fall into one of several stages of the buying process.

An *inquiry response* brochure is written to provide more information in response to another promotion, such as a television commercial or a print ad. These brochures provide many details about whatever is being marketed and are aimed at someone who has already shown interest. Inquiry response brochures include information about how to purchase whatever is for sale.

Point of purchase brochures are placed adjacent to an item that requires detailed information about its use. For example, a brochure showing the steps necessary to apply decorative paint might be placed near a store's display of paint products.

Sales support brochures are compiled to provide sales staff with comprehensive information about the product or service. They can be used during a sales pitch to illustrate a product's features or benefits. Other times, sales support brochures are called "leave behinds" because a salesperson will leave the brochure at the end of a sales call to act as a reminder about the product.

Content

Step One: Research

You must know your product inside and out before you can write one word about it. This means *research*. Good writers begin this process by immersing themselves in the product, service, or organization. Visit a factory if you are writing about a product. If you are writing about a group, go to the organization and interview members. Watch how something is done until you understand enough about it so you can to explain the process clearly.

Gather all preexisting written materials—ads, web copy, testimonials, press kits, and audiovisual materials. The writer must fully understand all aspects of a product or service, the way that product or service is viewed in the marketplace, how the competition measures up, and the strengths and weakness of the product or the service. Without this background information, creating an effective brochure will be impossible.

Successful brochures integrate the *features* and *benefits* of whatever is being promoted. *Features* are the physical characteristics of an item (or the activities and mission of an organization). A *benefit* is how a feature adds value to a product. For example, some pens have retractable nibs. The benefit of that feature is that it prevents ink from leaking. A feature of membership to an art museum is that members may view exhibits before they open to the general public. The benefit is that members do not have to stand in line or fight crowds to view exhibits.

A helpful way to understand the difference between features and benefits is to create a features and benefits table. Doing so provides the writer with concise words and phrases to use to write copy. Table 4.1 is a sample features and benefits table for Headphonies, a three-inch portable speaker that plugs into MP3 players or portable gaming devices.

The next part of research involves conducting a thorough analysis of the strengths, weaknesses, opportunities, and threats involved. This is known as a SWOT Analysis. Strengths and weaknesses are internal, that is, inherent to the product or service. Opportunities and threats are external and are beyond the control of the manufacturer or organization.

Let's say you are writing a brochure for a travel destination, New Orleans, intended to promote a specific tour, product, or event. You need to know what draws people to the city and what affects their decision to visit. This requires knowing all the features and benefits of travel to New Orleans as well as its strengths and weaknesses as a destination. It is wise to create a SWOT analysis for your product whether it is a location, a bar of soap, a service, or a group. Table 4.2 is an example of an abbreviated SWOT analysis of New Orleans as a destination.

From the SWOT analysis, the writer would build an even more specific list of points to be aware of when creating the brochure copy. For example, if research has shown that potential visitors are worried about criminal activity or subpar services in the aftermath of Hurricane Katrina, the writer needs to note that the city is functioning better than ever. If we know potential visitors are interested in food and architecture, it makes

Table 4.1. Features and Benefits of Headphonies

Features	Benefits
Small, compact, lightweight	Carry it anywhere
Cute, trendy designs	Choose your design to match your personality
$24.95 price	Affordable and less expensive than alternate speakers

Table 4.2. SWOT Analysis of New Orleans

Strengths	Weaknesses
Unique architecture and charm World-class restaurants Varied hotel options Fun, party atmosphere with many events (Mardi Gras, Jazz Festival)	Perceived danger and criminal activity Depressing aftermath of Katrina Perceptions that services are under par
Opportunities	**Threats**
French quarter charm intact after hurricane—good deals abound Abundant home, garden, and food reality shows may attract visitors to the unique offerings	Hurricane season could deter visitors from planning visits Economic downturn has affected travel

sense to feature photographs of unique Cajun and Creole dining options in the picturesque, quaint French Quarter.

The final step before writing brochure copy is to complete a *project brief*, a document that defines the goals and parameters of a copywriting task. One of the most important elements in the project brief is the idea of a *primary message*. A primary message is the one main point that must be conveyed. It is the heart and soul of a brochure.

To market a Southern Hemisphere beach destination to Americans during the U.S. winter, the primary message might be "When it's winter in the United States, it's summer in Brazil." The copywriter bolsters that main idea with *key support points*. These are features and benefits of travel to the destination as defined in Table 4.1 and the SWOT analysis (Table 4.2). A sample of a project brief appears at the end of this chapter.

Step Two: Copywrite

Writing copy for a brochure differs from writing news releases or newsletters. First of all, brochure images are as important as the prose, so the copy must work in tandem with the visuals. Second, some brochure writing (such as that for glitzy sales pieces) requires copywriting skills adopted from advertising. On the other hand, informational brochures work best when they do not use overly flowery prose or exaggerated claims to make a point. The writer must be aware of these stylistic differences when writing a brochure.

Style

Writing a successful brochure requires a distinct writing style character-ized by finesse and profound control of words. While some brochures are used to inform, ultimately they must persuade the reader to act in some fashion. Writers need to be aware of these tools and strategies before they tackle brochure copywriting.

Conciseness. Brochure writing uses a strategy called *chunking*. Chunking arranges information into bite-sized portions with headings and subheadings, short paragraphs, and short, easy-to-follow sentences. Since space is at a premium when writing brochures, copy must be tightly edited to omit all unnecessary words and redundancies. Use the strategies for omitting wordiness described in chapter 1 when you write and edit your brochure.

Conversational tone. A brochure uses a casual style to inform and persuade. The prose should flow naturally, as it does in a conversation. As we have discussed, the best way to attain fluid prose is to read copy aloud so you can hear and edit sentences that begin the same way, are choppy, or are lengthy and hard to follow. Work toward a mix of long, short, and medium-length sentences that avoid jargon. Rely on hard-working nouns and verbs that communicate more directly than flowery adjectives and adverbs. Feel free to begin sentences with conjunctions such as "and" or "but."

Parallelism and bullet points. Parallelism is a writing strategy used by all good copywriters. Parallelism means matching nouns with nouns, verbs with verbs, and phrases with phrases. Readers expect parallelism, especially in sets of two or three items. Using parallel phrasing sets up expectation in the reader and, when used correctly, delivers a punch the reader will appreciate.

Often, brochures use a list formation to supply information suc-cinctly. When doing so, writers frequently organize the material into bul-leted points. When listing items, always use parallel structure. If using a verb to begin the first point, use a verb for every point. The same goes for a noun or a phrase.

Positive voice. Brochure copywriters use positive words to make a point. Instead of saying "New Orleans is no longer dangerous" a copy-writer would emphasize the positive and say, "Enjoy nonstop fun in

America's most vital and unique city." An accompanying photo might show a couple strolling at night on Bourbon Street or a family posing with a policeman in front of Saint Louis Cathedral. Avoid negative words or phrases that can convey an unfavorable connotation, and rephrase in a positive way. Instead of "No discounts will be honored after May 1," say "Discounts will be honored through April 30."

Use of "you." Using the second person is a good way to achieve a conversational tone when writing a brochure. When using "you," remember the writer is speaking directly to the reader, so save this technique for appropriate topics and audiences.

Organization

According to copywriting guru Robert Bly,[1] the order in which people look at brochures is as follows:

1. Heads and subheads
2. Special offers (if provided)
3. Illustrations and captions
4. Body copy in order of reader interest

Note that brochures are not read in a linear fashion. But copy must be organized logically, which means the brochure must be written in a linear fashion; we cannot just haphazardly lay down information. There must be a natural flow of ideas.

When organizing a brochure, think about how your audience will read it. Sort information logically so readers can easily locate points. Begin by creating an outline with details that become headings and subheadings. Under these, jot down how you will explain or deliver on the promise of the heading.

Since you won't know how many pages the brochure will be until you have completed the copy, write your copy before laying out the design (unless your budget dictates a size.) Aim for tightly edited prose to minimize cost; brochures should only be as long as they need to be. Be complete, but use as few words as possible.

Cover. Brochure covers must draw in the reader two ways: with a compelling visual that communicates as much about the brochure topic as possible and with a title or name that explains the topic. Say you are creating a brochure to encourage parents to vaccinate their children. The cover photo might include a happy mother and baby and a title such as "Protecting Your Baby: A New Mother's Guide to Vaccinations."

Figure 4.1 is the cover of an informational trifold for a high school art program that features student artwork and the organization's name. Its colorful, artistic design emulates a portfolio review and invites readers to learn more about the program.

Many brochure covers also include a snappy *slogan*, also referred to as a *tag line*. Tag lines are a great way to emphasize the main selling point or advantage being illustrated. While tag lines come to be identified with a product or service in an organic way, they take lots of trial and error to create. If you decide to create a tag line, begin by jotting down everything you can think of that is beneficial about the organization, product, or service. Whittle down your list to five of the most important aspects, and then hone in on the one you want to emphasize. From there, distill your message into a pithy, memorable saying. Shorter is always better than longer!

Back. Readers often ignore the back of the brochure, so it should not contain any major information. The backs of many brochures simply list the firm's contact information and logo. If the brochure is being used to sell, make sure the back includes all the information the customer needs to carry out the next step in the buying process. Using the earlier New Orleans example, the back cover might tell the reader, "Contact your travel agent or call us at 123-456-7890 to book your trip today!"

Inside. The brochure's guts are broken into panels. Brochures with multiple pages will have several panels per page, and those panels can be vertical, horizontal, or a combination of both. If using more than eight pages, include an index so the reader will know where to find specific information. Write your brochure as a series of short sections, each with a head or subhead.

The inside front panel (or page) is the most read portion of a brochure. In a persuasive brochure, this panel can include key selling points or a testimonial from a satisfied customer. For an informational brochure, the inside front panel can include FAQs about an organization or "Important Tips" on a "how-to" brochure.

The content of the inside front panel should be distinct from the *inside spread*. Inside pages describe the product or organization, highlighting

Figure 4.1. Cover of trifold brochure.

customer benefits. Rather than listing features, the inside spread should emphasize how the product, service, or organization meets the needs and wants of the reader. Inside, organize the information in the way your reader will likely respond best. In the case of our vaccination trifold, the inside copy might be broken down into a series of questions that act as headings:

- What are vaccines?
- Why does my baby need vaccines?
- Are vaccines safe?
- When should my baby get vaccines?
- How will my baby react to vaccines?
- Do vaccines have side effects?

Notice how the organization of the questions mirrors a story with a beginning, middle, and end. And from simply reading the headings, the reader understands the brochure's story line. The story may be "Three easy steps to choosing your next dishwasher" or "Ten facts you need to know when traveling abroad," but the answers tell a story to a reader who needs to know these answers. The brochure delivers complete information written in a clear, entertaining style that is not overtly self-serving and that shows that the writer understands the readers' needs.

Figure 4.2 is the inside spread of an informational brochure about gestational diabetes and illustrates how to use columns and headings effectively.

Headings and Subheadings

The headings and subheadings tell the brochure's story. A reader should be able to understand the gist of the content from examining heads and subheads. But boring heads can be counterproductive. Try to be reader oriented when writing headings; think about which reader benefit you can emphasize rather than which point you can illustrate. For example, instead of "About MarketPros," say "How MarketPros Delivers." Use words that pack a punch.

Try parallel headings. If you are using questions, use them throughout. If you begin each heading with a gerund, the *ing* form of a verb

How do I know if I'm at risk?

Answer the questions below to learn your risk level* for gestational diabetes.

	Yes	No
1. Are you a member of a high-risk ethnic group *(Hispanic, African American, Native American, or Pacific Islander)*?	○	○
2. Are you overweight or very overweight?	○	○
3. Are you related to anyone who has diabetes now or had diabetes in their lifetime?	○	○
4. Are you older than 25?	○	○
5. Did you have gestational diabetes with a past pregnancy?	○	○
6. Have you had a stillbirth or a very large baby with a past pregnancy?	○	○
7. Do you have a history of abnormal glucose tolerance?	○	○

If you answered **YES to TWO or more** of these questions, you are at **HIGH RISK** for gestational diabetes.
If you answered **YES to ONLY ONE** of these questions, you are at **AVERAGE RISK** for gestational diabetes.
If you answered **NO to ALL** of these questions, you are at **LOW RISK** for gestational diabetes.

Should I get tested?

If you are at...	Your health care provider will*...
High Risk	Test you as soon as you know you are pregnant. If the first test is negative, he or she will likely test you again when you are between 24 and 28 weeks' pregnant.
Average Risk	Test you when you are 24 to 28 weeks' pregnant.
Low Risk	Probably not test you unless you start to have problems.

Keep in mind that every pregnancy is different. Even if you didn't have gestational diabetes when you were pregnant before, you might get it during your current pregnancy. Or, if you had gestational diabetes before, you may not get it with this pregnancy. Follow your health care provider's advice about your risk level and getting tested.

What if I don't get treated for gestational diabetes?

Most women with gestational diabetes have healthy pregnancies and healthy babies because they control their condition. Without treatment, these women are at risk for: high blood pressure, preeclampsia (a sudden, dangerous increase in blood pressure), and fetal death during the last 4 to 6 weeks of pregnancy. These women may also have very large babies. Some women need surgery to deliver their bigger babies, which can increase the risk of infection and prolong recovery time.

As babies, children whose mothers had gestational diabetes are at higher risk for breathing problems. As they get older, these children are also at higher risk for obesity, abnormal glucose tolerance, and diabetes.

These women and their children also have a higher lifetime risk for type 2 diabetes. It may be possible to prevent type 2 diabetes through lifestyle changes. Talk to your health care provider about diabetes and risk from gestational diabetes.

What is gestational diabetes?

Gestational diabetes (pronounced jes-tay-shun-ul die-uh-bee-teez) is a type of diabetes, or high blood sugar, that only pregnant women get. In fact, the word gestational means pregnant. If a woman gets high blood sugar when she's pregnant, but she never had high blood sugar before, she has gestational diabetes. Nearly 200,000 pregnant women get the condition every year, making it one of the top health concerns related to pregnancy.

If not treated, gestational diabetes can cause problems for mothers and babies. Some of these problems can be serious.

But there is some good news:

- Most of the time, gestational diabetes goes away after the baby is born. The changes in your body that cause gestational diabetes normally occur only when you are pregnant. After the baby is born, your body goes back to normal and the condition goes away.

- Gestational diabetes is treatable, especially if you find out about it early in your pregnancy. The best way to control gestational diabetes is to find out your have it early and start treatment quickly.

- Treating gestational diabetes greatly lower the baby's chances of having problems.

Figure 4.2. Inside brochure pages.

used as a noun (e.g., "Choosing Your Baby's Doctor" and "Watering Your Orchid"), make all the headings gerunds.

Subheadings are subordinate to the heading under which they fall. If you use subheads, make sure the reader understands they are related to the heading and that all subheads mirror each other graphically. Like the lines on an organizational chart, heads and subheads should have equivalent weights. This can be achieved with a graphic device such as a color, font, or shading.

Visuals

Brochures marry words with images to create meaning and to stimulate action. Visuals in a brochure must be meaningful rather than extraneous and are used to illustrate a key point related to the primary message. Knowing when and which visual to use is a specialized skill. For this reason, many firms employ a graphic designer to lay out brochures.

Sometimes existing visuals must be used. In that case, the writer must work around whatever is available. Remember that it is illegal to download copyrighted images. Your company may be sued if illegal use of an image is discovered.

Matching visuals to content. The type of visual used depends on what is being communicated. In general, brochures contain photographs, charts or graphs, diagrams, illustrations, and maps.

Photographs should be used to show a product in action. Imagine a brochure about a car without an image of that car driving on the road. Sometimes a firm will hire a photographer to shoot a product so it is professionally lit, or even go on location to shoot the product. A good photograph is as important to a successful brochure as good copy.

Some brochures use *illustrations, diagrams,* or *drawings* in lieu of photographs. For example, if writing a brochure about atherosclerosis, a gory photograph of a clogged artery would be difficult to understand; an illustration better communicates the concept. In some cases, a diagram or illustration must be used. No photograph can illustrate the food pyramid, for example.

Charts and *graphs* are the clearest ways to illustrate data. *Bar charts* are used to compare items. For example, a bar chart could be used to differentiate between the increase of male and female smokers over a given time period or show year-end earnings from two divisions. *Pie charts* show parts of a whole. A pie chart is a good way to illustrate the components of an advertising budget or where membership monies are allocated. A *line chart* or graph shows changes over time. Perhaps you want to show how earnings have increased since 1990. A line chart helps the reader visualize this data. A *flow chart* illustrates a process or a procedure.

Maps are used to illustrate location. Most travelers will want to view the route of a tour; in this case, a map would be critical. If you want to illustrate a business's location, you might include a street map rather than written instructions. Remember to omit unnecessary information when using a map as an illustration. Show only what the reader needs to see.

Design and Layout Basics

Designing a brochure can be a highly creative endeavor requiring mastery of graphic design applications such as Photoshop and Adobe Illustrator. It can also be quite simple; an 8½ × 11" trifold can be designed in many word-processing applications. Whichever way you go, design the brochure *after* writing the copy.

The following are a few design basics to keep in mind as you write.

Color. Brochures can use one color (usually black and its permutations of gray), two-color (black and one other color), three-color (black and two other colors), or four-color, meaning the full color spectrum. Typically, brochures with color are more expensive than black-and-white brochures. But using a four-color format gives photographs depth and realism and provides designers with more choices. When using color, be aware that some colors are difficult to read. For example, try reading yellow type for any length of time! Stick to black or dark colors for most of your copy. If you want to use color for headings, make sure they are readable. And do not go overboard; pick a color scheme of two or three colors at the most.

Font. Type fonts are divided into two basic types: *serif* and *sans serif*. Serif fonts such as Cambria, Times, Garamond, and Courier have "feet and tails" that create a line of sorts to help the eye track, which is why most novels, newspapers, and other material with dense words use serif fonts for copy. Sans serif fonts like Calibri, Helvetica, Arial, and Verdana do not have the feet and tails on serif fonts and feature a more modern, clean look to them. (Notice how the 12-point font appears different in each of the previous examples. This is because of something called the font "x-height," which is the height of a font's main body.)

Sans serif fonts create a clean line that makes them eye-catching for headings and more easily read on a computer screen. But reading lots of type in a sans serif font can tire the eyes. Many designers use sans serif fonts for headings and a serif font for body copy. Bear in mind that font styles connote meaning; Chili Pepper is playful and fun, but no one would want to read an annual report written in it!

Odd shapes. A way to make a brochure stand out is to use an odd shape. A brochure for gardening tools in the shape of a trowel may encourage readers to pick up the brochure and buy a product. The problem is cost. An odd-shaped rather than standard-sized brochure requires die cutting, which is expensive to produce.

Placement of copy. When laying out a brochure, consider two page-design basics. One is the *"Z" pattern*. Because English is written from left to right, readers look at the upper, left-hand side of a page first and use a "Z" pattern to follow narrative. The points of the "Z" are natural spots upon which the eyes rest, so designers place less important text on those areas. The second is to view a page as a *grid*. Each page is a blank sheet that can be divided into various sections or grids. A four-page, 8½ × 11" brochure has an inside "blank" of 17 × 11"—requiring several different grids or columns. Think of grids as ways to separate ideas you express in your copy. A grid can be differentiated with color, rules, lines, photographs, or other graphic devices.

Paper. Paper choice affects printing quality and price, so the type of paper a brochure is printed on matters. Thin paper will bleed color; heavy, glossy stock will be difficult to fold. Colored paper will affect photographs and readability. A good printer will know the pros and cons of various paper choices and can help you understand these distinctions early in the design process.

White space. Space without illustrations or copy is referred to as *white space*. Some designers lay out pages with a lot going on; others prefer clean lines with plenty of white space. While no formula exists for deciding on a good balance between clutter and white space, remember to keep messages visible and to think of how the reader will react to the visual design.

Conclusion

Brochures, because of their staying power, continue to play an important part of any firm or organization's promotional mix. From a simple photocopied trifold to an intricate 16-page splash on glossy stock, brochures illustrate a company's message and are often a consumer's only point of contact with an organization. Taking the time and effort to design a brochure that effectively meets readers' needs will result in an invaluable component of a company's public persona.

Project Brief

Project name:

Project description: What needs to be produced? (½ page B&W ad; 4-page, 4-color brochure, etc.)

Background: Describe what research has been uncovered about the product, especially in relation to competition. Describe the competitive arena and any specific communication situations that may be encountered.

Primary message: What is the *single* primary message?

Primary benefit: What is the target audience's *single* primary benefit?

Key support points: What features and benefits will be used to support the primary message?

1.

2.

3.

4.

Tone: What overall tone should this project convey?

Marketing objectives: What marketing objectives are we trying to achieve?

Target audience: Who are the readers, viewers, and customers of this project? Describe any needs and perceptions they have about the product.

Current target audience perceptions: What is the audience's current attitude about what this project addresses?

Desired response: What do you want the target audience to do or think as a result of the project?

Mandatory elements: List specific images, logos, phone numbers, and so on that must be included in the project.

CHAPTER 5

Writing Web Copy

Today a website is as important as a company logo. Often a website is a member or customer's first impression of an organization, so a professional, easy-to-navigate, well-designed, and clearly written website is a basic business necessity. But because reading on a screen differs from reading on a printed page, web writers face distinct challenges.

Web writing differs from print writing in several significant ways. First, when writing for the web, the writer is typically part of a team. Websites integrate technology with copy, so writers collaborate with web designers, software engineers, and other members of an organization who have input into the site's content and usability. Another difference is that web writers use media such as sound and video as well as two-dimensional graphics and integrate these elements into copy. This blending of technology with words requires writers to think about their task in new ways.

Web Audience Analysis

Sites are designed with a specific audience in mind, whether it is broad (such as the audience for CNN.com) or specific and narrow (such as a site geared to cardiac surgeons or IT specialists). So as with every writing task, writers must consider their audience. Are the readers teenagers who have grown up with a mouse in hand or are they elderly people who have trouble reading small print? To best provide a site's readership with an optimal experience, the writer must know readers' limitations and expectations.

All web readers share a few common needs: They visit a site for information, whether that is a treatment option or an exercise regimen. And they all expect to access that information fast. If readers don't find what they need quickly, they will leave a site.

But beyond those similarities, readerships will vary greatly. A detailed reader's profile will help a web writer create a site that will be more successful in attracting and keeping readers. Begin the audience analysis portion of the first stage of the writing process (assessing) by completing Table 1.1 in chapter 1. But when writing for the web, go beyond those basic steps and create several *personas*[1] using the facts you've gathered about the site's readership.

A persona takes demographic data and actually creates a narrative about the typical user. This persona may include a photograph of a representative user, information about why the user visits the site, quotes gathered from interviews about using the site, and the user's web habits. A persona is similar to a novelist's character sketch and can be very useful when thinking about who is reading a site's copy. Use the "Persona Template" at the end of this chapter to help you create a persona for your user.

Many organizations conduct *usability tests* to assess a site's effectiveness. These tests are designed to measure the user's experience, including ease of use, error frequency, and satisfaction. Conducting a usability test can be as simple as sitting down with a user and watching how he or she navigates a site or as complicated as conducting surveys or focus groups. The savvy writer will consider usability test results when evaluating web copy.

A final point: It is important to remember that the web is indeed "worldwide." Audiences from Japan to Jamaica can access an organization's website. So while we may have a specific reader in mind when we write copy, we must also be aware that our readership is entirely out of our control unless a site is password protected. If you are writing sensitive material, be aware that anyone, anywhere can—and likely will—read it.

Determining Purpose

As we have discussed, websites primarily provide information, which calls for an objective, clear, and concise writing style. Yet many sites are also designed to persuade visitors to purchase a product or service. Visitmexico.com (http://www.visitmexico.com/wb/Visitmexico/Visi_Home ?show=regions) is clearly a site dedicated to providing information to potential tourists. But that information is designed to persuade readers to choose Mexico as a vacation destination. It does so by offering complete, factual information arranged in layers that are intuitively organized and written in a concise, easy-to-read format.

Some sites exist solely to entertain and are written in a distinct style to serve the site's audience. For example, the mock political news site *The Onion* is sarcastic; the entertainment site *E! Online* is gossipy. When a site's audience expects an attitude or voice, the writer must deliver.

Reading on the Screen Versus on the Printed Page

Reading on a printed page differs from reading on a computer screen. Reading on a screen takes nearly 25% longer than reading a printed page.[2] Most traditional print copy is read in a linear fashion, from beginning to end. But because of a website's interactivity, readers jump from page to page. This type of reading is called nonlinear—readers select a section and click to read it.

Readers tend to scan web pages and sites, focusing only on what interests them. To organize a website to meet this expectation, writers categorize copy into a series of headings in an organization style called *hierarchical branching*,[3] which can be likened to an outline with headings and subheadings.

As readers scan, they have definite expectations about web copy, the most basic of which is *speed*. They want to "get it" as fast as possible, so web prose needs to be clear and concise. Speed also refers to the length of time a page takes to load; as broadband capabilities have improved, readers have come to expect pages to load almost instantly. If a page takes too long to appear, readers quickly lose interest and click away, often out of a site entirely.

Web readers also expect a site to have *visual logic* and *organization*. Although usability experts do not agree about how many clicks is too many to find a piece of information, they do agree that a site's organization must be intuitive—that is, readers must be able to seamlessly access information. Readers access information in layers, so the writer must organize web pages accordingly. Finally, web readers expect information to be updated regularly; sites with stale information lose credibility with today's readers.

Web Writing

A writing strategy called *chunking* works best when composing for nonlinear reading. As was discussed in chapter 4, chunking arranges information into bite-sized portions of about one hundred words so they can fit on

one computer screen without requiring scrolling. Chunking is typified by
abridged paragraphs and short, easy-to-follow sentences. To appeal to web
readers' need for speed, web copy must be tightly edited for conciseness and
efficiency. A basic rule to follow is to halve what would be written for print.[4]

Site organization. A website's "face" is the *home page*. The home page
should immediately express the site's purpose and set its tone or personality
with colors, graphics, writing style, and visual elements. Readers don't spend
much time on a home page, so its material should be organized intuitively,
allowing visitors to quickly access information or begin tasks. The example of
the home page in Figure 5.1 illustrates this organizational approach.

Figure 5.1. Home page.

Montecito Bank and Trust's home page provides a clear snapshot of the site's offerings.

The home page provides links to *destination* or *information* pages, often via a *pathway* page.

A destination page (sometimes called an information page) contains the information the reader seeks. Each destination page should have a clear title so when visitors arrive, they immediately know they are in the right place. Figure 5.2 is a destination page from the same organization previously illustrated.

A *pathway page* is an intermediary page that guides readers to a specific information page. This type of page can be likened to a table of contents[5] and is often just specific headings containing links to information pages. Often this approach is used by large organizations whose websites contain many layers of information.

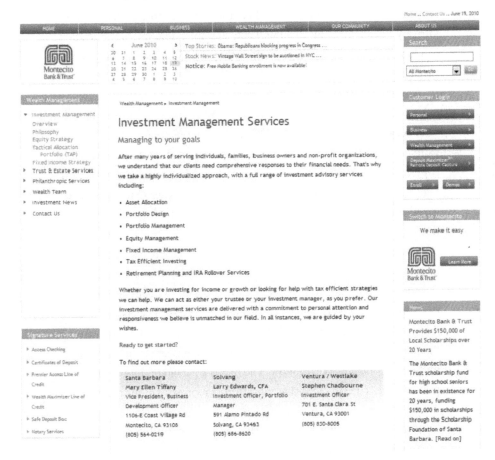

Figure 5.2. Destination page.

Source: http://www.montecito.com/Depts/Wealth/Default.aspx

When developing web copy, it's important to have a clear picture of the site's organization. A *site map* is a graphical overview of a website, showing hierarchical relationships between pages. Before writing website copy, create this map and define the routes your readers will have to take to obtain specific information.

Most websites are arranged with *navigation tabs* on the top of a page. For example, on the home page for Visitmexico.com, we are greeted with colorful tabs labeled "About Mexico," "Destinations," "Activities," "Vacation Theme," "Travel Experiences," and "Events." The left side of the home page has links to both the same destinations as the tabs and additional ones. When the visitor clicks "Activities," a destination page with four subheadings lists 30 options. The reader may choose to delve deeper into any one of them by clicking. Each clickable, descriptive subheading contains another layer of information that is obtainable by clicking the specific page.

A well-organized site is key to its success and includes the following elements.

Scannability. Because web readers scan rather than read word for word, effective web copy is written to meet this need. To create scannable copy, highlight words that capture main ideas. That being said, too many highlighted words create a blur that will confuse rather than aid readers. Avoid long blocks of type; keep paragraphs short, aiming for no more than eight lines. Limit the number of characters per line to 70 for optimum scannability (a character is a letter, punctuation mark, or space); lines longer that those with 70 characters are hard for the eye to track.

Another technique to make text scannable is to use *bulleted points* and *headings*. Bulleted lists make text scannable because readers can glance down a list much faster than they can read a dense paragraph containing the same information. For example, look at the difference in scannability in the two paragraphs that follow. The first is a paragraph intended for the printed page. The second is that same information written for the web.

Santa Barbara's temperate weather and unique history make it an ideal destination. Just 150 miles north of Los Angeles, Santa Barbara boasts many cultural and recreational attractions for the whole family to enjoy. Begin with a tour of the historical landmarks in the downtown area and take in the Presidio and Mission, both built in the 18th century. Santa Barbara's Botanical Gardens feature native plants and magnificent vistas, and the harbor offers whale watching cruises. Enjoy the outdoors on pedal go-carts, or take a kayak off Stearns Wharf. Surf, golf, or horseback ride, or take a day trip to Santa Barbara's picturesque wine country or nearby, Dutch-themed Solvang.

Santa Barbara's ideal weather and history make a great destination, with cultural and recreational activities such as:

- Historical tours of Presidio and Mission
- Botanic Gardens
- Harbor cruises and whale watching
- Biking
- Golf
- Kayaking
- Horseback riding
- Day trips to Solvang or wine country

Each bulleted point in the second paragraph would be a link that the visitor could click to obtain another layer of information. Notice the number of words in the second paragraph is reduced by more than half, and the selection is easy to scan.

Headings and *subheadings* also help readers scan text. By breaking text into blocks labeled with a heading that summarizes the content, the reader can easily focus on specific areas of interest. *Subheadings* are miniheadings[6] that break up long text, mostly to enhance visual appeal. Headings and subheadings should be short and indicative, explaining the subsequent content with specificity. Use nouns and verbs, and avoid cutesy headings meant to entertain rather than inform. Many headings and subheadings omit articles (a, an, the) if doing so does not compromise meaning.

Interactivity. Integrating various media into a website can make it dynamic and interactive. When composing web copy, the writer should think about how words can mix with visuals to enhance meaning. Various media are available: sound, video, animation, or images. All are accessed using links. Links are similar to visual aids used in a speech or items in an appendix of a written report. It's worth noting that too much media interspersed within text can detract from meaning. Graphics and sound should be inserted to enhance meaning, not simply because it's technologically possible to do so.

Interactivity poses another challenge. If you provide a link that takes users outside of your site, they may never find their way back. Another negative of links that send readers out of your site is that some sites evaluate their effectiveness by "stickiness," or how long a user stays on a page or in a site. If a link sends readers away from the site, the stickiness factor decreases.

Page length. Because web readers are typically in a hurry, they're less likely to scroll down a page to read more information. If you cannot limit a web page to one screen, consider providing *anchors*. Anchors are headings that appear at the top of a page and link to sections or subheadings within a long page. Anchors provide another way to help web readers get where they want to go faster.

Web Writing Style

Web writing demands economy above all. Impatient readers have millions of website choices, so websites need to be concise and clear. The following elements should be considered as you write web copy.

Inverted pyramid structure. When writing web copy, organize material according to the inverted pyramid style we discussed in chapter 3. Begin with the most important information, which is summarized in the first paragraph. Arrange subsequent information in descending order of importance. Since readers may not scroll down, keep critical information to one screen and be aware that only readers who are very interested in a topic will stick with it long enough to scroll down several panels.

Paragraph length and style. While all writers need to be aware of how words appear on a page, web writers must be particularly sensitive to the visual aspect of their copy. Keep paragraphs short to avoid dense blocks of text. Break up paragraphs with bulleted lists and use highlighting to emphasize key words.

For maximum usability, build paragraphs written for the web around one idea. And just like your English teacher taught, begin the paragraph with a topic sentence. The reason is simple: Often web readers will only read the first line of a paragraph.

Web writers sometimes use spacing to emphasize a point. For example, to draw attention to an important idea, the writer may use a one-sentence paragraph. This journalistic technique works well on the screen but should be used sparingly.

Sentence length. It may be surprising to learn that a sentence of as few as 20 words is considered difficult to read; a sentence of seven words is considered easy. Knowing that web readers are busy and impatient, writers need to be aware of sentence length as a way to simplify web copy. Aim for sentences of between 10–20 words at the most. Avoid long, rambling sentences with embedded phrases such as this:

> A person working out for the first time should be monitored by an experienced trainer, who has either been licensed or who has been involved in the exercise business for a long enough time to be knowledgeable about the body, and should be aware that muscle soreness and aches are to be expected.

The sentence revised should read as follows:

> People new to exercise should be monitored by an experienced, licensed trainer and can expect some muscle soreness.

While web copy should aim for shorter rather than longer sentences, your writing still needs to be rhythmical and conversational. Avoid series of short, choppy sentences, and always read web copy aloud to make sure it flows and just sounds right.

Professionalism. A site with grammatical errors and typos screams *unprofessional.* One of the first things teachers warn students to watch for when analyzing a website's credibility is typos. Other signs of unprofessional (and therefore noncredible) sites are broken links, dated information, and authors who do not provide their credentials. Professional sites are carefully edited, and any errors are fixed immediately.

Tone. A site's personality is reflected in its writing voice or tone. A key characteristic of web copy is its conversational tone, so it's entirely appropriate to use "you" when talking to your user. In so doing, you will also avoid passive voice and extra words.

A website's tone depends on its level of formality. For example, a site for a global organization would demand a professional tone with precise, correct English. Such a site would avoid fluffy language, rambling sentences, and words with emotional connotation or denotation. A small, local business might emphasize a more casual, neighborly tone to appeal to nearby residents.

Sites dedicated to selling a product may use a persuasive, marketing-style approach that relies on exaggerated claims, generalizations, high-pressure language, and superlatives.[7] Websites using these strategies abound, and many are probably successful. Some consumers undoubtedly respond to high-pressure techniques ("Buy now—limited time offer!") and over-the-top claims. Here's a perfect example taken from Hoodia.com.

Make your brain think your [*sic*] full with Hoodiamax and lose 1–6 lbs per week!

The fact that the claim includes the wrong form of a word ("your" instead of "you're") might turn off some readers, but many will ignore or be unaware of the error and be taken in by the unsubstantiated claim. Still, savvy web users would click away from such a site quickly; more and more users are knowledgeable about how to evaluate web content for accuracy. Additionally, many people find "salesy" language a turnoff and prefer objective explanations of a product or service when conducting research. Use caution with obvious sales-driven phrasing.

Word choice. Simple, well-known words work best for web copy. If text requires technical language and a portion of the intended audience is nontechnical, define the jargon. For example, if writing about a medical condition for a lay audience, the writer might word an explanation like this:

Cardiac infarction—also called a heart attack—is the number one killer of women.

When in doubt, choose the simpler word or term.

Conclusion

Web writing requires understanding the unique needs of web readers. Because the web audience needs to access information quickly, the writer must be especially sensitive to clarity and conciseness. Web writers must also be familiar with basic usability strategies to create meaningful, effective websites. The web also provides writers with almost endless possibilities to embed other media within their words. This unique capability makes web writing distinct from other media we've discussed.

Persona Template

Name	
Photo	
Occupation	
Web habits	
Quotes	
Knowledge level (specific to product/ organization)	
Goals (specific to product/ organization)	
Needs/wants	
Skills	
Narrative	

CHAPTER 6

Writing for Social Media

Blogs and Microblogs

The new world of social media has added another layer to the marketing and public relations mix. With the proliferation of social networking and video-sharing sites, blogs, and chat rooms, the web is crawling with online commercial communication. Successful marketers have caught on to the enormous potential these new media platforms provide and are making social media a vital part of their marketing mix.

This chapter will focus on two arenas of social networking: *blogs* and *microblogs*. Blogs—short for web logs—are sites written by an individual with a special interest in a topic as a way to share that interest and point of view with others.[1] Blogs provide interactivity by allowing readers to post comments in response to what the blogger writes, thus creating community. Organizations use blogs to communicate directly with consumers, bypassing the established media entirely.

Microblogs are shorter than traditional blogs. They may be published using technologies other than the web-based methods and include text messaging, instant messaging, email, or digital audio. Among the most notable microblog services are Twitter, Tumblr, Plurk, Emote.in, Beeing, Jaiku, and identi.ca.

The popular Twitter microblogs called "tweets" are limited in length to 140 characters. With 75 million users and counting, Twitter has become increasingly popular with organizations as a way to reach a network instantly, thus creating word-of-mouth publicity. Social networks allow a message to be viewed immediately by thousands and thousands of readers, making the posts invaluable—when they work.

Audience Analysis

Social networking has two main audiences: customers and clients and the media.

Customers and clients. Current or potential customers and clients are a primary audience for blogs and tweets. People interested in an organization, a product, an issue, or a person form the target audience for many content-specific blogs and tweets. These readers are a niche audience who are actively looking for input.

Since a majority of blogs and tweets are aimed at an organization's current customers or clients, these readers should be well defined, whether the posting organization is a global leader such as Starbucks or a start-up looking to attract new customers. As with all writing tasks, writing for social media will be most effective if the content fits the needs and wants of the target audience.

To create a more intimate and successful relationship with readers of blogs and tweets, the writer should create one or several *personas* for these messages. As we discussed in chapter 5, a persona is a profile or an invented biography of a typical user or buyer. For example, a PR professional working for a university might create several personas as targets for social networking that could include newer alumni, older alumni, prospective students, or parents. Each persona has specific needs that could be targeted in the posts.

It's also a good idea to monitor the activity of your competitors' blogs and tweets to understand your audience. By watching the discourse between a competitor and its audience, you may gain important feedback that will influence your communication.

Use Table 1.1 and the Persona Template in chapter 5 to help define your audiences for blogs and tweets.

Media. The media is the second audience for an organization's social networking efforts. Editors and writers comb the web in search of ideas for stories, interesting people, and news about organizations. Social networking conversations provide the media with fodder for good copy, thereby allowing an organization to reach an otherwise fickle audience. And for unknown organizations, using free networking can be a way to attract the media's attention. By following a social media community's comments about a product or an organization, the "legitimate" media can pick up on a new trend and write about it. In the eyes of the media, simply having an audience validates an organization or its product.

Determining Purpose

Blogs and microblogs are designed to provide useful, consistent, and interesting updates that create and engage a community of people who share a concern or need. The goal of these media is to establish a readership that ultimately becomes an audience for a product, provides immediate customer feedback, and creates a communication tool for handling any negative news. In this way, social media is similar to direct mail campaigns—but without the cost of postage.

The following provides an example of how an organization might use social media as part of its public relations campaign. Say a bicycle shop owner in Portland, Oregon, starts a blog geared to bicycling enthusiasts. One blog post might include a link to a video from the *Tour de France* simply to share with like-minded enthusiasts. Our bicycle shop blogger might post another blog that offers news about an upcoming local bike race with links for more information about how to participate. To announce the blog, the shop owner might send a tweet informing its network that a new blog has been posted with a link to the post. And finally, when the bike shop has an upcoming promotion, the blogger will inform the community of the opportunity with a blog post and a tweet. The blogs would reside on the bike shop's website with archived older posts.

Interactive and informative blogs and tweets can be highly effective channels of communication that produce a lot of bang for a relatively low cost.

Content

As we've discussed, blogs and microblogs must be informative to attract savvy readers. Therefore, content must appeal to the readership's interests. The information in a blog might be news or commentary, but readers of these messages always expect an interactive experience. Therefore, part of each message includes a link to video clips, photographs, other blogs, publications, or websites. Unlike a website, however, a blog is dynamic, changing several times each week.

Characteristics of blog writing. Because blogs are a way to humanize the dialogue between a company and its potential users, their writing voice is extremely casual. Blogs should read like a conversation with someone who has a distinctive voice. Consequently, any graphical element (such as underlining or italics) or turn of phrase that helps the blog "sound" like a conversation is not just allowed—it's expected.

Before jumping in and writing, spend some time observing the online community's conventions. Look for commonly used acronyms, jargon, and stylistic elements such as tone and language use. If you're going to become a member of a group, you don't want to stick out—you want to fit in.

The following are some of the basic characteristics of blog writing:

- Catchy, intriguing headlines
- Keywords that contain the blog's main idea; searchable words for search engine optimization (SEO)
- Graphical devices such as *italics*, dashes (—), and punctuation marks (!) for emphasis or to emulate a real conversation
- Length of several paragraphs to 300 to 400 words
- Short sentences that avoid long introductory phrases or dependent clauses
- One-sentence paragraphs or very short paragraphs
- Questions sprinkled throughout
- Pull quotes to highlight a theme or catchy phrase to draw in readers
- Links to other sites
- Casual tone with relaxed adherence to conventional grammar
- Careful balance of information share and self-promotion
- Artwork or some sort of graphic for visual interest
- "About Me," a brief author bio, and a photo or other icon representing the organization

Note: Although blogs take a relaxed approach to correctness, no organization wants to be considered sloppy or careless. At the very least, make sure to spell check a blog post!

Characteristics of tweets. Tweets help an organization or an individual create an online presence. Those who follow a Twitter account are interested in a particular subject and therefore anticipate tweets as a way of keeping posted and up to the minute. But because tweets are limited by length, they share certain characteristics:

- No headline
- Profile picture, company logo, or a photo of an individual's face or a product (subject to change if one doesn't produce results)
- Questions to prompt engagement
- Length of up to 140 characters, or roughly 12 words
- Truncated language that omits articles ("a," "an," "the") and abbreviations
- Link to a recommended URL; using a URL shortener such as bit.ly
- Content containing a response to another tweet, a recommendation, or a link to an item of interest
- Exclamation points (!) and question marks (?)
- Writing style similar to news headlines

Interconnectivity of Social Media

The various elements of social media—blogs, tweets, and social networking sites—can work in tandem and with the organization's other marketing tools. For example, the organization's website will have a tab to its blog and a link to sign up to receive the group's newsletter. The organization will notify its network of new blog posts or other news via tweets. Still another social media tool that is quickly gaining popularity is a social network page, with Facebook being the current favorite choice. Other popular social networking websites include MySpace, LinkedIn, and XING, with each having its own microblogging feature, better known as **status updates**.

Facebook pages allow organizations to create an online presence that engenders interactivity among "fans" or readers. Organizations are increasingly using this free new media device to keep a community engaged. Smaller organizations especially can make use of the free analyticals Facebook provides that measure traffic and reader demographics. Facebook pages help brand an organization and are yet another way to communicate with potential clients. They mirror blogs and tweets in that they too are conversational and interactive and provide pertinent information to readers. Writers should use the same language on all social media for branding purposes and to stay on message.

Conclusion

Social media is quickly becoming an essential part of every organization's marketing mix. But because it's a fast-growing, new PR tool with no fixed model to follow, newcomers may be wary of jumping in. The upside is that nothing created in social media is etched in stone. A tweet can be deleted; a fan post can be edited; a comment on a blog can be taken down. In the interactive world, nothing is forever, so mistakes can be covered up.

One thing is for certain. Writers who master the language and technology of social media will have an increasingly valuable part to play in the organization's public relations strategy.

CHAPTER 7

Media Kits

PR professionals are routinely called on to put together media kits, a collection of materials providing facts about an organization, its leadership, its products, an event, or an issue. As the name denotes, media kits are intended for use by the media and should not be confused with packets designed for sales support. Although a kit put together for sales may contain many of the same elements as a media kit, its purpose is entirely different.

Media kits are used to supply the media with background about an organization or the necessary facts to cover an event. That event may be a speech given by an organization explaining a product recall (think Toyota); it might be an introduction to a new product (think iPad); it might be a public relations disaster (think BP in the Gulf). In all cases, the organization would provide a media kit containing salient information.

Traditional media kits are hard copy, but increasingly this is changing. Some organizations provide digital versions of a print media kit in PDF format. Many organizations simply post information on their websites that is accessible to any interested party. The benefit of this approach is that information can be updated regularly, thereby making it more timely and less expensive than a print media kit. Still, the hard copy media kit continues to be a staple of the PR function.

Media Kit Audience

Media kits are put together to provide information to those in print, radio, television, or Internet-based media. As we have previously discussed, editors and reporters form an uneasy alliance with public relations practitioners; both need one another to exist, but both are skeptical of the other's motives. Knowing this, the PR professional must serve the organization while not antagonizing or alienating the media. The contents of a media kit should be well written to appeal to a discerning audience and objective to appeal to this audience's sense of ethics.

Media Kit Purpose

Media kits are designed specifically to provide background material a reporter or news entity needs to cover an event or feature a subject in an article or radio or television broadcast. Therefore, this material should be complete, well written, factual, and objective. Nothing will make a reporter less inclined to write a good story than a self-serving media kit.

Media Kit Appearance and Contents

The materials in print media kits are placed into an attractive one- or two-pocket folder. An image of the product being promoted or the company's logo is often affixed to the cover. The stock quality, cover image choice, and printing of these folders all work to create an image. A folder with a glossy, four-color photograph and metallic touches connotes a glitzy event or product, whereas a folder made of high-quality stock with matte finish and embossed with a company logo produces a more conservative image. Folders vary vastly in price, but if kept simple can be relatively inexpensive to produce.

Often organizations print a large number of folders to have on hand for various purposes. Sometimes the folder is designed to be multifunctional. Other times an organization may create a separate folder for a specific event. In both cases, this shell for the contents is the first thing the media sees and should be created with the tastes and needs of the media in mind. All folders should include a die cut in which a contact person's business card is placed.

The contents of media kits vary but all tend to include the following:

1. **Fact sheets**. A tersely written overview, the fact sheet has bold-faced headings and bulleted points. It may include an overview of the organization with names of principals, number of employees, address, location(s), contact information, and the like. A fact sheet may be about a new product with product specifications; it may

provide the facts of an upcoming event. It will answer the standard news questions: who, what, where, when, and why.

2. **News releases**. The specially prepared news release about the event or subject may be accompanied by previous pertinent news releases.

3. **Bios**. A one-page description of each of the organization's main players accompanied by a headshot of reproducible quality. Bios can be straightforward and simply discuss the executive's experience and accomplishments at the organization, or they can be narrative and include more personal details.[1]

4. **Nonprint items**. If broadcasters are covering the event, they will require a video. Print media will need photographs. Visuals should be included in the media kit and be produced with the media's needs in mind.

5. **Backgrounder**. The backgrounder provides an explanation of the mission, history, and strategic vision of an organization written in paragraph style with an objective tone. This document can go into depth about the organization, even explaining day-to-day operations.

Optional items or those items that would only be included for a specific event include the following:

1. **White paper or position paper**. A *white paper* is a technical report that educates readers about an issue or a topic. A *position paper* is opinion based and conveys an organization's stand on an issue.

2. **Past news articles**. Any time an organization has had press coverage, the organization has tear sheets of those articles reproduced. These are often included in a media kit to illustrate that the organization has been worthy of media coverage.

3. **Spokesperson's statement**. A spokesperson's statement is a quote or quotes from an individual speaking on behalf of the company or organization designated to go on the record. These include the spokesperson's contact information.

4. **Pitch letter**. Pitch letters are persuasive letters to an editor or writer of a specific media vehicle proposing an idea for a story. (This is discussed in more detail later in the chapter.)

The organization and placement of the items in a media kit should be logical and easy to follow. If there are many pieces, a list of included items similar to a table of contents could be used. In addition, the media might find it helpful to have all the materials reproduced on a CD, which should also be placed in the folder.

When I worked at a software firm, we had a media kit area in our offices. In it were dozens of printed pieces in separate slots. These pieces included various news releases, reprints of articles about the firm and its leadership, product information sheets, brochures, director bios, and more. These sheets were available to the staff for both sales and marketing purposes. It was a popular spot!

Pitch Letters

A pitch letter is crafted to capture the interest of the most jaded of readers: an editor or reporter. Pitch letters are used by organizations to prod an editor or reporter to cover a story featuring the organization's product, service, or event. For example, a foreign country might hire a U.S. PR firm to raise awareness of its nation. As part of the overall PR strategy, the PR representative might write a letter to a travel magazine writer or editor hoping that the idea pitched in the letter would stimulate interest in writing about the destination.

If it sounds impossible, it's not . . . but it *is* difficult! Good pitch letters contain an angle that will appeal to both the editor *and* the readership or viewing audience. A successful pitch requires not just thinking the way the media thinks but also understanding that media's needs.

Pitch letters work best when the PR professional analyzes the publication (or television show) to understand the type of stories that are typically covered. Back issues or shows should be read or viewed to make sure the idea has not been done previously. Target a writer or producer who specializes in covering stories related to the idea being pitched. The better the background research, the better the chance the idea will be picked up.

A good pitch letter is tightly written and error free and includes the following elements:[2]

- Name of specific individual to whom the idea is being pitched.
- A professional tone. Don't become effusive or imagine that you are the writer's pal. That will just irritate a journalist.
- A first paragraph that reads as if it were the lead of the article; it should hook the reader with its captivating, feature article style.
- A second paragraph that describes how and why the story will appeal to the readers or viewers of the particular media, illustrating an understanding of both the publication or show and the reader or viewer.
- A third paragraph that provides the terms of the offer: Is the story an exclusive? If so, for how long will you hold it? Discuss how you can help with setting up interviews or obtaining original art. Do *not* offer to write the story!
- The date by which you'll need to have a definitive answer. Be polite and thank the addressee.
- A sign-off with a simple "Sincerely."

The sample in Figure 7.1 illustrates how a PR writer might pitch an idea to a writer.

Conclusion

Media kits continue to be indispensable in public relations. Whether they are sent as a PDF or handed out at an event, media kits are versatile tools that help an organization promote its message. As with all writing for public relations, media kits require the writer to be acutely aware of the audience's needs while simultaneously serving the organization's purpose.

April 13, 2011
Mr. John Doe
Staff Writer
Travel on a Budget
11111 Park Place
New York, NY 10001

Dear Mr. Doe:

Brad Smith and his buddies are such hardcore campers that they plan their monthly weekend getaways a year in advance. But after repeatedly visiting the same old location near their homes in San Diego, they needed a new spot. The guys were pretty picky, though. Brad insisted on pristine hiking trails. Mario needed clear streams with plenty of fish. They all wanted rugged bicycle paths and untouched natural surroundings. Then Brad found Idyllwild. And things got a little, well, wild! Did I mention the bear? Never mind, the story has a happy ending.

I think readers of *Travel on a Budget* would enjoy hearing about the camping adventures of Brad and his friends in the little-known gem of Idyllwild, California. Nestled halfway between LA and San Diego in the San Jacinto Mountains, Idyllwild gave these working men a weekend they'll not soon forget. Such an article would complement your recent series on weekend getaways in Northern California and would appeal to active readers who want to learn about affordable destinations with lots of exciting activities.

We can offer you this story as an exclusive and provide you with access to Brad and his colorful camping cohorts as well as exquisite still and video footage of Idyllwild's natural surroundings, but I'd have to know your intention by [date]. We even can give you a shot of Brad and the bear! Please give me a call at 555–111–1234 or email me at *xxx@xxx.com* to let me know if I can be of any help.

I'll follow up with you on [date] to see how I might be able to assist you. Thanks for your consideration.

Sincerely,
[Name, Position]

Figure 7.1. Sample pitch letter.

Notes

Chapter 1

1. Guffey (2008), p. 103.
2. Guffey (2008), p. 103.
3. Guffey (2008), p. 103.

Chapter 2

1. Newsom and Haynes (2011), p. 155.

Chapter 3

1. Diggs-Brown (2007), p. 112.
2. Diggs-Brown (2007), p. 112.
3. Newsom and Haynes (2011), p. 294.

Chapter 4

1. Bly (1990), p. 167.

Chapter 5

1. Redish (2007), p. 19.
2. Nielsen (2000), p. 101.
3. Garrand (2006), p. 111.
4. Nielsen (2000), p. 101.
5. Redish (2007), p. 54.
6. Newsom and Haynes (2008), p. 290.
7. Jeney (2007), p. 118.

Chapter 6

1. Scott (2010), p. 37.

Chapter 7

1. Diggs-Brown (2007), p. 71.
2. Marsh, Guth, and Short (2005), p. 51.

References

Bly, R.W. (1985). *The copywriter's handbook*. New York, NY: Henry Holt & Company.

Diggs-Brown, B. (2007). *The PR style guide* (2nd ed.). Belmont, CA: Wadsworth, Cengage.

Garrand, T. (2006). *Writing for multimedia and the web* (3rd ed.). Burlington, MA: Elsevier.

Guffey, M. (2008). *Business communication: Process and product* (6th ed.). Mason, OH: South-Western Cengage.

Jeney, C. (2007). *Writing for the web: A practical approach*. Upper Saddle River, NJ: Pearson-Prentice Hall.

Marsh, C., Guth, D., & Short, B. (2005). *Strategic writing*. Boston, MA: Pearson.

Newsom, D., & Haynes, J. (2008). *Public relations writing: Form & style* (8th ed.). Belmont, CA: Thomson-Wadsworth.

Newsom, D., & Haynes, J. (2011). *Public relations writing: Form & Style* (9th ed.). Boston, MA: Wadsworth.

Nielsen, J. (2000). *Designing web usability*. Indianapolis, IN: New Riders Publishing.

Redish, J. (2007). *Letting go of the word: Writing web content that works*. San Francisco, CA: Elsevier.

Scott, D. (2010). *The new rules of marketing & PR*. Hoboken, NJ: Wiley.

Index

The letters f and t following a page number denote a figure or table.

Announcing the Business Expert Press Digital Library

Concise E-books Business Students Need for Classroom and Research

This book can also be purchased in an e-book collection by your library as

- a one-time purchase,
- that is owned forever,
- allows for simultaneous readers,
- has no restrictions on printing, and
- can be downloaded as PDFs from within the library community.

Our digital library collections are a great solution to beat the rising cost of textbooks. e-books can be loaded into their course management systems or onto student's e-book readers.

The **Business Expert Press** digital libraries are very affordable, with no obligation to buy in future years.

For more information, please visit **www.businessexpert.com/libraries**. To set up a trial in the United States, please contact **Sheri Allen** at *sheri.allen@globalpress.com*; for all other regions, contact **Nicole Lee** at *nicole.lee@igroupnet.com*.

OTHER TITLES IN OUR CORPORATE COMMUNICATION COLLECTION
Series Editor: **Debbie D. DuFrene**

Lightning Source UK Ltd.
Milton Keynes UK
UKHW021501171022
410614UK00012B/2267